Becoming Christ's
Children of the Covenant

Becoming Christ's Children of the Covenant:

Understanding God's Plan for the Salvation of Man

Douglas T. Bentley

CFI
Springville, Utah

ISBN: 1-55517-837-5
e.1

Published by Cedar Fort, Inc.
www.cedarfort.com

Distributed by:

CEDAR FORT

Typeset by Natalie Roach
Cover design by Nicole Williams

Printed in the United States of America
10 9 8 7 6 5 4 3 2 1

Printed on acid-free paper

Dedication

To Deonn, without whose loyalty I would not have been able to accomplish this project.

CONTENTS

Preface

I have been a teacher of the restored gospel of Jesus Christ for the past three decades, and as I have observed people both young and old during this time, one thing has become increasingly clear to me. We, as members of Christ's restored Church, The Church of Jesus Christ of Latter-day Saints, need a deeper understanding of the gospel of Jesus Christ if we are (1) to gain our own exaltation and (2) to effectively gather scattered Israel so they can gain their exaltation as well.

As I have listened to the Brethren of late, those impressions have been deepened upon my mind. Elder M. Russell Ballard, in October conference of 2002, gave one of the most pointed talks I have ever heard on these matters. During his talk, he made this timely statement: "We don't need spiritually weak and semicommitted young men. We don't need you to just fill a position; we need your whole heart and soul. We need vibrant, thinking, passionate missionaries who know how to listen to and respond to the whisperings of the Holy Spirit. This isn't a time for spiritual weaklings. We cannot send you on a mission to be reactivated, reformed, or to receive a testimony. We just don't have time for that" ("The Greatest Generation of Missionaries," *Ensign,* November 2002, 47).

What he said, in essence, is that there isn't time for our young men to wait until they go into the mission field to gain their testimonies or to learn the doctrines of the gospel. They must do it now, before they go.

All I have to say to that statement is amen! I think Elder Ballard hit the nail on the head. How can we possibly think to accomplish such an awesome task as fulfilling one of the greatest prophecies recorded in scripture without arduous preparation? I feel strongly, however, that his message applies not just to the young men in the kingdom of God. We have all been commanded that when we have been warned, we are to warn our neighbor. As members of the tribe of Ephraim, we are all to be missionaries, at all times and in all places.

This Church has been able to confound the mighty with the level of success it has had in gaining converts to its ranks by sending out weak things of the world, as many of us are, including our green and unseasoned missionaries. This is an undeniable witness to me of the Church's truthfulness. Somebody once said that if the Church weren't true, the missionaries would have wrecked it a long time ago. Although this statement was made in jest, I believe it is true. When I think of the growth that the Church has made since its restoration in 1830, I can't help but wonder what we have done to the Lord's timetable because of our lack of knowledge and preparation.

A friend recently asked me, "Wouldn't you like to be able to go back into the mission field, knowing what you know now?" I replied, "Yes, and I fully intend to, just as soon as I'm able." There is no greater work that we can perform in this life than serving our fellowmen by helping them gain their eternal exaltation. The scriptures tell us, "For behold, this is my work and my glory—to bring to pass the immortality and eternal life of man" (Moses 1:39).

What would happen if every member of our Father in Heaven's family really understood just who we really are, and claim to be, as members of the Church of Jesus Christ? What if every member of the Church had a sound doctrinal knowledge and a burning conviction of the restored gospel? What then?

According to an apostle of the living God, the time has come for the gospel to be taken to the four corners of the earth by emissaries who are not themselves still in search of their own epiphany. The Lord wishes to share with each of us His mysteries: "Wherefore, I will explain unto you this mystery, for it is meet unto you to know even as mine apostles" (D&C 19:8).

"Behold, it has been prophesied by our fathers, that they should be kept and handed down from one generation to another, and be kept and preserved by the hand of the Lord until they should go forth unto every nation, kindred, tongue, and people, that they shall know of the mysteries contained thereon" (Alma 37:4).

Nevertheless, the Lord is not just going to open the windows of heaven and pour out all of this wondrous light upon us without any effort on our part. The Savior has said, "Wherefore lay apart all filthiness and superfluity of naughtiness, and receive with meekness the engrafted word, which is able to save your souls. But be ye doers of the word, and not hearers only, deceiving your own selves" (James 1:21–22).

I firmly believe that the average member of The Church of Jesus Christ of Latter-day Saints has a testimony of the divinity of the Book of Mormon and of the Prophet Joseph Smith. That is what has pushed this work along with such success for so many years. But if I am hearing the Brethren right, the time of being average members of the Church is over. One of the Lord's modern apostles, Neal A. Maxwell, once said something to the effect that "all of the easy things the Lord has had for the Church to do are done. From now on it's high adventure" (*Wherefore Ye Must Press Forward,* 84). That is a mind-boggling statement when we consider what those "easy things" were. If what the Church has gone through is easy, I think we'd best strap on our spurs and get ready for quite a ride!

If we are going to accomplish the work that our Savior has for us to do to usher in His second coming, we cannot afford to be average Latter-day Saints any longer. I feel that we are held back by fear of accomplishing what our Father intends for us to accomplish—fear caused by our lack of a working knowledge of what we as a Church really know to be true. We know the Church is "the only true and living church upon the face of the whole earth, with which I, the Lord, am well pleased, speaking unto the church collectively and not individually" (D&C 1:30).

When it comes to being able to clearly explain to a person who is not of our faith what we really believe from a doctrinal standpoint, I sense that most of us feel grossly inadequate.

My intention in this work is twofold. First, I hope to provide a down-to-earth resource for each person who desires to know of the truthfulness of The Church of Jesus Christ of Latter-day Saints and its doctrine. Second, I hope to give confidence to all who have desires to explain the great plan of salvation to others. The responsibility of all who have entered into sacred covenants, through baptism and the other saving ordinances, is to be a witness of God at all times, in all things, and in all places (Mosiah 18:9). I hope that this work will help us fulfill our sacred obligation, as the tribe of Ephraim, to gather the lost and scattered house of Israel and bring them home to the source of their exaltation.

Introduction

It is through making and honoring covenants that God, our Heavenly Father, reclaims His spirit children. The Father chose a specific lineage as His chosen people, and if any of us expects to live with Him again and dwell forever in His presence, we must partake of the covenants that He has outlined for us in the Old and New Testaments. Not one of us will leave this mortal existence clean and pure, free from sin and spotless. Only one Person was capable of that distinction, and that is why He was able to qualify as our Savior. The law of eternal justice demands, therefore, that each of us dwell somewhere other than where He and His Father dwell.

By becoming partakers of the covenants that our Savior outlined in the holy scriptures, we can become members of His adopted family and, therefore, partakers with Him of the blessings of eternal life. The law of mercy allows those of us who truly humble ourselves and turn our lives and our wills over to the Savior to enter into our Father's rest, despite our human shortcomings.

As the Savior's adopted sons and daughters, we become children of the covenant. As such, He will grant us a pardon from our sinful lives if we repent and come unto Him. Only those who are of the covenant will be allowed to pass by the angels who will stand as sentinels and enter into the rest of God.

Christ is our advocate with the Father and, as such, will, in essence, say: "Father, these are my family, and though they have had their shortcomings, I will cover them. Please allow them to enter with me into your glory." It is through the making and keeping of those covenants with Him that we can lay claim to that grace. It is through the Savior's grace, and only through that grace, that we can be saved from the eternal reward that we have merited in mortality. It is a gift from Him, not something that we earn but something that we must qualify for by our actions, by becoming His covenant family.

This book is an attempt to outline, in a simple format, the whole grand plan that was formulated in the heavens long before we were born into mortality and that is put into place for each of us when we are born into this life. Once we understand this great plan and the purpose of the holy scriptures, we learn how and why we make required covenants. This book explains the process of becoming Christ's children of the covenant.

Chapter 1
The Eternal Nature of Man

And there stood one among them that was like unto God, and he said unto those who were with him: We will go down, for there is space there, and we will take of these materials, and we will make an earth whereon these may dwell; and we will prove them herewith, to see if they will do all things whatsoever the Lord their God shall command them; and they who keep their first estate shall be added upon; and they who keep not their first estate shall not have glory in the same kingdom with those who keep their first estate; and they who keep their second estate shall have glory added upon their heads for ever and ever.

—Abraham 3:24–26

Before we came to earth to begin our mortal sojourn, we lived as spirit children of our Father in Heaven. He begat us, and we walked and talked with Him, just as we do here with our earthly parents. He desired for us to grow and develop and become as He is, just as our earthly parents should. He developed a plan whereby this task could be accomplished. It would require that each of us go through a mortal experience. We would, in a sense, suffer a spiritual death by being out of our Father's presence during that experience. We would need to come to earth and take upon ourselves physical bodies of flesh and blood. These bodies would be subject to human frailties, sickness, disease, and, ultimately, death. Through this mortal experience, we could gain valuable experience that would enable us to become like our Heavenly Father.

For such a plan to work, however, a number of elements were required. First, an environment would need to be created that would be conducive to our gaining the desired experiences. Second, eternal principles and laws would need to be followed. A grand council was held in the heavens during our premortal existence, and we each had our say in the matter.

Our Father's plan required that each of us come to earth and begin anew, helpless and totally dependent upon others for our survival. We would be subject to pain, suffering, sickness, and death. We would face the possibility of bad choices, which would subject us to sorrow—something we had not previously experienced. We would be out of our Father's presence and be required to make decisions that would directly affect the quality of our existence. It would be possible that we might pursue a course that would make our temporary separation from Him a permanent one. One eternal law that would need to be met was that for each act of willful rebellion (sin) committed by us here on earth, atonement would be required. Sin is defined in the scriptures as knowing good and doing it not (James 4:17). Only one who was free from sin and disobedience and who would be willing to ransom those who were not free from sin could make this atonement. Each of us who successfully returned to our Father from this mortal test would bring honor and glory upon Him, for we are His creations.

One premortal spirit, Lucifer, opposed our Father's plan. He proposed his own variation to that plan. His version would guarantee the return of all of our Father's spirit children to Him. It would include force and would not allow for choice or mistakes. The danger of failing to return would be removed, but so also would the inherent growth that would come from making our own decisions and choices. One other major change included in this counterfeit plan would be that Lucifer, not the Father, would gain the glory.

One who met the required criteria for making the Atonement in the plan laid out by our Father then stepped forward and asked that He be sent to pay the ransom. He would submit His own will to that of the Father and carry out the Father's plan. He would also set the terms that would go along with this recompense. Those terms would require that each of us enter into a contract with Him and accept Him as our creditor, accepting also of our own free will and choice the terms of such a contract.

It was put to a vote, and two-thirds of our premortal family sustained our Father's grand plan. Lucifer, whose plan was rejected, rebelled. In anger, he mounted a campaign against the Father's plan, and war raged in heaven. Satan was persuasive, and he succeeded in drawing away the "third part" of the spirit children of the Father after him (Revelation 12:4). In his wrath Lucifer swore vengeance against our Heavenly Father and against all of us who chose to follow our Father's plan. As a result of this rebellion, he became Satan, the devil, the father of all lies, and he, along with all those who chose to follow him, were cast down, never to obtain a physical body of their own. These fallen spirits, along with their general, were defeated and cast out of our Father's presence. They were then designated to dwell eternally in outer darkness at the conclusion of this earth's mortal experience. An account of this pre-earth war in heaven is recorded in the book of Isaiah:

> How art thou fallen from heaven, O Lucifer, son of the morning! How art thou cut down to the ground, which didst weaken the nations!
>
> For thou hast said in thine heart, I will ascend into heaven, I will exalt my throne above the stars of God: I will sit also upon the mount of the congregation, in the sides of the north: I will ascend above the heights of the clouds; I will be like the most High.
>
> Yet thou shalt be brought down to hell, to the

> sides of the pit. They that see thee shall narrowly look upon thee, and consider thee, saying, Is this the man that made the earth to tremble, that did shake kingdoms;
>
> That made the world as a wilderness, and destroyed the cities thereof; that opened not the house of his prisoners?
>
> All the kings of the nations, even all of them, lie in glory, every one in his own house.
>
> But thou art cast out of thy grave like an abominable branch, and as the raiment of those that are slain, thrust through with a sword, that go down to the stones of the pit; as a carcase trodden under feet. (Isaiah 14:12–19)

With the casting out of heaven of Lucifer and his followers, however, the war had just begun. Those who were cast out were intent on destroying all of us who chose to come to earth. They will do all in their power to destroy the souls of men and keep them from returning to the presence of their Father in Heaven. Their tool is rebellion. Their ally is darkness. They are cunning and ruthless. They appear to be harmless as doves but are as dangerous as vipers. They are wolves in sheep's clothing (see Matthew 7:15), bloodthirsty and bent on the destruction of the entire human family. They have no conscience and seek that everyone might become miserable like unto themselves. Because they will have no mortal body, they do all in their power to "rent" one of ours for a time. In fact, so great is their craving for a physical body, they will even take that of a pig (Matthew 8:28–34).

Because our Father in Heaven knew of their plan to destroy us, He limited their ability to influence us. The only way they can prevail upon us is if we give them the power to do so. We empower them by enlisting with them in their rebellion. Our Father in Heaven operates in the light, contrary to Satan, who is at his evil best when he can cloud our light with his cloak of darkness. His goal is to steal light from the spirit sons and daughters of our Father in Heaven (1 Corinthians 4:5; D&C 93:39). We are successful in avoiding his designs only to the extent that we are obedient to the counsel of our Father.

Darkness repels light. In fact, darkness is merely the absence of light. When we walk in darkness, it is difficult for us to see what surrounds us. Therefore, if the father of darkness can get us out of our true Father's light, the possibility of our stumbling and becoming disoriented and lost is enhanced. The more each of us does to obey our Father's plan, the more light He is able to shed on us.

> He that ascended up on high, as also he descended below all things, in that he comprehended all things, that he might be in all and through all things, the light of truth;
>
> Which truth shineth. This is the light of Christ. As also he is in the sun, and the light of the sun, and the power thereof by which it was made.
>
> As also he is in the moon, and is the light of the moon, and the power thereof by which it was made; as also the light of the stars, and the power thereof by which they were made;
>
> And the earth also, and the power thereof, even the earth upon which you stand.
>
> And the light which shineth, which giveth you light, is through him who enlighteneth your eyes, which is the same light that quickeneth your understandings;
>
> Which light proceedeth forth from the presence of God to fill the immensity of space—
>
> The light which is in all things, which giveth life to all things, which is the law by which all things are governed, even the power of God who sitteth upon his throne, who is in the bosom of eternity, who is in the midst of all things. (D&C 88:6–13)

The sad fact, however, is that many of our Father's children love darkness more than they love light (John 3:19). Earth's battleground is cluttered with the souls of those who are "walking in darkness at noon-day"

(D&C 95:6, 12; Isaiah 59:9–10). The more light we allow ourselves to walk in, the more clearly we can discern the hellish tactics of the evil plan of the adversary.

How then were we to know those things that we would need to do to walk in that light and avoid the pitfalls of that darkness? Our Father, in His loving mercy, built that path into His earthly plan for us as well. In His infinite wisdom, He would include disseminators of that light to guide and direct us during our earthly sojourn. These men would be called prophets. They would be His mouthpiece and representatives to us. Whenever He would have us know something, He would communicate that information to mankind through these chosen vessels (Amos 3:8). If we would follow the words and counsel of these chosen inspired men, we would be able to walk in our Father's light and thus navigate our way through the earthly darkness of the adversary.

Father Adam was the first of these prophets. In the premortal existence he was known as Michael, and he was heavily involved in the planning of the creation of this earth. He was to be followed by other noble and great ones, such as Seth, Enoch, Noah, and others, many of whom would stand at the head of the various gospel dispensations. Whenever God's children became wicked enough to warrant taking His gospel and power from them, a gospel dispensation would end. When the time was right, a new prophet would then be called to restore the gospel again in its fullness to the people in the following dispensation.

God would also afford those of His children who would enter into and abide by covenants access to the constant companionship of the third member of the Godhead, the Holy Ghost. In addition to the physical words of the chosen prophets, the Spirit would provide an indelible impression upon our minds of divine truths. This guidance, if followed, would help us avoid earthly pitfalls. Between the promptings of the Spirit and the counsel of the holy prophets, anyone who truly wished to could safely navigate their way through mortality. Extra help would also be extended to us through entering into sacred covenants. Through these covenants, empowerment would be given through the holy priesthood. This priesthood, the power by which our Father and the pre-mortal Savior conducted their affairs, would be extended to worthy men who were willing to enter into a sacred covenant to obtain and honor it. This priesthood would authorize men to act in God's name and have their acts be recognized by Him as legal and binding. The priesthood covenant was all-important to facilitate the Father's plan of happiness for His spirit children in their mortal existence.

The Father chose a man of true obedience to accomplish the priesthood covenant. His name was Abram. After proving this chosen servant to see if he would be obedient at all costs, the Father revealed to him (and us) just what that process would be. The Father changed his name from Abram to Abraham and established a covenant with this great patriarch—a covenant that would be perpetuated through his posterity, thus enabling them to know of the Father's true way back into His presence. He was told that through his seed all of the families of this earth would be blessed. That covenant was passed down through Abraham's son Isaac, and in turn to his grandson whose name was Jacob. The Father reestablished the covenant with Jacob and then changed his name to Israel. It was through Israel's posterity that the blessing of the whole earth would be carried out. For this promise to be fulfilled, it would require that all members of the human family align themselves with this chosen family. To them, and only to them, was given the key to returning to the Father's presence.

Authority was bestowed upon this designated family, and ordinances were required of the Father's children before they could be allowed back into His presence (John 3:5). That authority was paramount in the plan because it would be through that authorization that the entire plan would be administered. The ordinances would be accompanied by covenants that must be entered into by all of us, just as Abraham, Isaac, and Jacob had done, if we are to qualify for salvation.

A saving atonement would be required on behalf of all those who would be guilty of sin. As members of the human family, we would be required to humble ourselves, repent of our wrongdoing, and submit to the conditions that were set forth by our Savior for our redemption. This Savior would pay the ransom for our willful disobedience. He would willingly suffer the price for our sin, and thus, we would be indebted to Him for our redemption and salvation. In a sense He would become our creditor and we His debtors. He agreed not only to suffer for our sins but also to die for us as well so that we wouldn't be relegated to the earthly grave as our eternal resting place.

This redemption would not be free but would require that we join with the covenant family, the house of Israel, in entering into those covenants and receiving those ordinances at the hands of our Father's duly authorized servants. If we were unwilling to submit to those conditions, we would not have complete access to the Savior's saving atonement. Agency was to be given to each of us to choose for ourselves our own eternal destinies, just as it was given to our first parents, Adam and Eve. If we chose to reject this offer of grace and mercy from our Savior, we would be required to pay the price for our own sins, thus negating the infinite sacrifice made by our brother on our behalf. As far as we were concerned, Lucifer would have won his battle for us. We were to be turned over to his buffetings and left alone to fare for ourselves.

This master plan was not the one with the most guaranteed returnees, but it was definitely the one that would allow for optimum growth and development for the Father's children. That was His desired goal.

At the end of our mortal life, we will be required to make an accounting of our earthly experience. Whether or not we want to believe that is irrelevant. We all come to earth the same—naked and crying, with a veil of forgetfulness over our minds. When we leave this earth, we will all leave in a similar fashion. We will take with us only what we have become—who we are. Whether we leave here crying or in a state of rest will depend upon the choices we have made concerning our Father's plan.

If we have chosen to seek the light that our Father has offered us, we will be received into a state of rest, joy, and happiness. This condition will be known as paradise and is reserved for the righteous. If, however, we have chosen to forsake the light and have instead sought the darkness offered by the adversary, we will enter a condition known as spirit prison. This condition will not be one of peace but rather one of weeping and wailing and gnashing of teeth. There we will be subject to the buffetings of Satan and will be required to suffer the price for all our unrepented sins. If we didn't learn to be obedient during our mortal existence, we will have plenty of time to learn it, for we will remain in this condition, also known as hell, until we have learned obedience.

When we have sufficiently learned that principle, we will be allowed to come out of hell but will remain in the spirit world until the end of the thousand years that Christ will personally reign upon the earth. At the end of these thousand years, known as the Millennium, our spirits will be reunited with perfected physical bodies, and we will be delivered before the Savior for our final judgment.

Those who remain in open rebellion against the Father and his teachings will then be returned to the bottomless pit to suffer an everlasting hell, prepared for the devil and his angels. On the other hand, those who have lived worthily and have taken the Savior as their redeemer will be rewarded with glory, immortality, and eternal life—the greatest of all the gifts of their Heavenly Father. They will be privileged to dwell with Him and His beloved Son eternally. They will enter into the rest of the Father. He will be their God, and they will be His children. This is the destiny of those who pass the test of mortality and return faithfully to the Father.

Chapter 2

The Creation

In the beginning God created the heaven and the earth.

—Genesis 1:1

And it came to pass that the Lord spake unto Moses, saying: Behold, I reveal unto you concerning this heaven, and this earth; write the words which I speak. I am the Beginning and the End, the Almighty God; by mine Only Begotten I created these things; yea, in the beginning I created the heaven, and the earth upon which thou standest.

—Moses 2:1

A while back I decided to try to learn a little more about my computer. I am what some would call computer illiterate, and I am not the kind of person who has a lot of spatial skills. I can build or put together just about anything if I can see it and get it in my mind, but don't ask me to follow the instructions! I decided that if I was ever going to understand the world of computers, I needed some real hands-on experience. It so happened that my computer was experiencing some glitches, and I didn't have money to take it to a technician. I have a teaching associate who got his bachelor's degree in computers and is fairly skilled in the computer field, so I went to him for some pointers. I didn't know a motherboard from an ironing board or a zip drive from a Sunday drive. I learned that there's RAM and CD ROM, processors, megabytes, gigabytes, and floppy discs. They are all run by something called a hard drive. I had a couple of older computers, so I proceeded to delve into their mysterious internal parts.

After a few hours of manual labor, I had successfully transferred the good hard drive from one computer to another computer whose hard drive had gone down. I "skillfully" put all of the cables back on the parts they had come off and was thinking to myself that computers weren't so complicated after all. I plugged my "new" computer in and prepared to admire my newly acquired skill.

Unfortunately, the computer wouldn't boot up. I returned to my mentor down the hall and petitioned for some additional help. He informed me that I would need to reload Windows. I had no idea where the old disc was. I thought I had done a pretty good job of assembling all of the components necessary to have a working computer (that is, except for the handful of small screws that I ended up with when I was finished). But in the end I realized that there is a lot more to creating a computer than just throwing a bunch of components together. I have occasionally pondered on that concept since then and have marveled at how someone was able to create the computer.

Just what would it take to assemble such a marvelous creation? I suppose that someone just took all of the different components, put them into a large box or bag, and then shook them up until they all fit together perfectly. I don't totally understand computers, but I am intelligent enough to know that such a process would be absurd. I also realize that even though I don't fully comprehend how to create a computer, others obviously do because I have one that enables me to reap the benefits of their skill and knowledge. Somewhere, somehow, someone created it, so I would be pretty naive to say that it couldn't be. I guess there are just some things that I, with my limited understanding, must choose to accept on faith. It doesn't really matter what I may think about it, truth is truth, and it is up to me to either accept it or reject it while I can see it.

In a way, that is how we can sum up the creation of this world we live upon. Man has concocted a number of different theories to explain its creation. One of them is the big bang theory. This theory claims, in essence, that all of the elements or components of this earth were put into a "test tube" and shaken up and then happened to all come together as we now have them. What an amazing coincidence! I, who am actually quite handy, had to tediously labor for hours to assemble a few man-made components in an attempt to build a computer, which still didn't work properly despite the physical assembly. What do you think the odds are, then, that the elements of this complex earth, with all of its diversity —its seasons, atmosphere, and grand design—could just magically come together and function as they do?

Let's discuss what the scriptures have to say about the Creation. Separate accounts of the Creation are found in Genesis, Moses, and Abraham. The biblical account appears adequate until we read the accounts in the other books. For comparison, let's read each one. First, from Genesis:

> In the beginning God created the heaven and the earth. And the earth was without form, and void; and darkness was upon the face of the deep. And the Spirit of God moved upon the face of the waters.
>
> And God said, Let there be light: and there was light. And God saw the light, that it was good: and God divided the light from the darkness. And God called the light Day, and the darkness he called Night. And the evening and the morning were the first day.
>
> And God said, Let there be a firmament in the midst of the waters, and let it divide the waters from the waters.

And God made the firmament, and divided the waters which were under the firmament from the waters which were above the firmament: and it was so.

And God called the firmament Heaven. And the evening and the morning were the second day. And God said, Let the waters under the heaven be gathered together unto one place, and let the dry land appear: and it was so.

And God called the dry land Earth; and the gathering together of the waters called he Seas: and God saw that it was good.

And God said, Let the earth bring forth grass, the herb yielding seed, and the fruit tree yielding fruit after his kind, whose seed is in itself, upon the earth: and it was so.

And the earth brought forth grass, and herb yielding seed after his kind, and the tree yielding fruit, whose seed was in itself, after his kind: and God saw that it was good. And the evening and the morning were the third day.

And God said, Let there be lights in the firmament of the heaven to divide the day from the night; and let them be for signs, and for seasons, and for days, and years: and let them be for lights in the firmament of the heaven to give light upon the earth: and it was so.

And God made two great lights; the greater light to rule the day, and the lesser light to rule the night: he made the stars also.

And God set them in the firmament of the heaven to give light upon the earth, and to rule over the day and over the night, and to divide the light from the darkness: and God saw that it was good. And the evening and the morning were the fourth day.

And God said, Let the waters bring forth

abundantly the moving creature that hath life, and fowl that may fly above the earth in the open firmament of heaven.

And God created great whales, and every living creature that moveth, which the waters brought forth abundantly, after their kind, and every winged fowl after his kind: and God saw that it was good.

And God blessed them, saying, be fruitful, and multiply, and fill the waters in the seas, and let fowl multiply in the earth. And the evening and the morning were the fifth day.

And God said, Let the earth bring forth the living creature after his kind, cattle, and creeping thing, and beast of the earth after his kind: and it was so.

And God made the beast of the earth after his kind, and cattle after their kind, and every thing that creepeth upon the earth after his kind: and God saw that it was good.

And God said, Let us make man in our image, after our likeness: and let them have dominion over the fish of the sea, and over the fowl of the air, and over the cattle, and over all the earth, and over every creeping thing that creepeth upon the earth.

So God created man in his own image, in the image of God created he him; male and female created he them.

And God blessed them, and God said unto them, Be fruitful, and multiply, and replenish the earth, and subdue it: and have dominion over the fish of the sea, and over the fowl of the air, and over every living thing that moveth upon the earth.

And God said, Behold, I have given you every herb bearing seed, which is upon the face

> of all the earth, and every tree, in the which is the fruit of a tree yielding seed; to you it shall be for meat.
>
> And to every beast of the earth, and to every fowl of the air, and to every thing that creepeth upon the earth, wherein there is life, I have given every green herb for meat: and it was so.
>
> And God saw every thing that he had made, and, behold, it was very good. And the evening and the morning were the sixth day. (Genesis 1:1–31)

Second, from Moses:

> And it came to pass that the Lord spake unto Moses, saying: Behold, I reveal unto you concerning this heaven, and this earth; write the words which I speak. I am the Beginning and the End, the Almighty God; by mine Only Begotten I created these things; yea, in the beginning I created the heaven, and the earth upon which thou standest.
>
> And the earth was without form, and void; and I caused darkness to come up upon the face of the deep; and my Spirit moved upon the face of the water; for I am God.
>
> And I, God, said: Let there be light; and there was light. And I, God, saw the light; and that light was good. And I, God, divided the light from the darkness.
>
> And I, God, called the light Day; and the darkness, I called Night; and this I did by the word of my power, and it was done as I spake; and the evening and the morning were the first day.
>
> And again, I, God, said: Let there be a firmament in the midst of the water, and it was so,

> even as I spake; and I said: Let it divide the waters from the waters; and it was done;
>
> And I, God, made the firmament and divided the waters, yea, the great waters under the firmament from the waters which were above the firmament, and it was so even as I spake.
>
> And I, God, called the firmament Heaven; and the evening and the morning were the second day.
>
> And I, God, said: Let the waters under the heaven be gathered together unto one place, and it was so; and I, God, said: Let there be dry land; and it was so.
>
> And I, God, called the dry land Earth; and the gathering together of the waters, called I the Sea; and I, God, saw that all things which I had made were good.
>
> And I, God, said: Let the earth bring forth grass, the herb yielding seed, the fruit tree yielding fruit, after his kind, and the tree yielding fruit, whose seed should be in itself upon the earth, and it was so even as I spake.
>
> And the earth brought forth grass, every herb yielding seed after his kind, and the tree yielding fruit, whose seed should be in itself, after his kind; and I, God, saw that all things which I had made were good; and the evening and the morning were the third day.
>
> And I, God, said: Let there be lights in the firmament of the heaven, to divide the day from the night, and let them be for signs, and for seasons, and for days, and for years;
>
> And let them be for lights in the firmament of the heaven to give light upon the earth; and it was so. (Moses 2:1–16)

And third, from Abraham:

And then the Lord said: Let us go down. And they went down at the beginning, and they, that is the Gods, organized and formed the heavens and the earth. And the earth, after it was formed, was empty and desolate, because they had not formed anything but the earth; and darkness reigned upon the face of the deep, and the Spirit of the Gods was brooding upon the face of the waters.

And they (the Gods) said: Let there be light; and there was light. And they (the Gods) comprehended the light, for it was bright; and they divided the light, or caused it to be divided, from the darkness.

And the Gods called the light Day, and the darkness they called Night. And it came to pass that from the evening until morning they called night; and from the morning until the evening they called day; and this was the first, or the beginning, of that which they called day and night.

And the Gods also said: Let there be an expanse in the midst of the waters, and it shall divide the waters from the waters. And the Gods ordered the expanse, so that it divided the waters which were under the expanse from the waters which were above the expanse; and it was so, even as they ordered.

And the Gods called the expanse, Heaven. And it came to pass that it was from evening until morning that they called night; and it came to pass that it was from morning until evening that they called day; and this was the second time that they called night and day.

And the Gods ordered, saying: Let the waters under the heaven be gathered together unto one place, and let the earth come up dry; and it was so as they ordered; and the Gods pronounced the dry land, Earth; and the gathering together of the waters, pronounced they, Great Waters; and the Gods saw that they were obeyed.

And the Gods said: Let us prepare the earth to bring forth grass; the herb yielding seed; the fruit tree yielding fruit, after his kind, whose seed in itself yieldeth its own likeness upon the earth; and it was so, even as they ordered.

And the Gods organized the earth to bring forth grass from its own seed, and the herb to bring forth herb from its own seed, yielding seed after his kind; and the earth to bring forth the tree from its own seed, yielding fruit, whose seed could only bring forth the same in itself, after his kind; and the Gods saw that they were obeyed.

And it came to pass that they numbered the days; from the evening until the morning they called night; and it came to pass, from the morning until the evening they called day; and it was the third time.

And the Gods organized the lights in the expanse of the heaven, and caused them to divide the day from the night; and organized them to be for signs and for seasons, and for days and for years; and organized them to be for lights in the expanse of the heaven to give light upon the earth; and it was so.

And the Gods organized the two great lights, the greater light to rule the day, and the lesser light to rule the night; with the lesser light they set the stars also;

And the Gods set them in the expanse of the heavens, to give light upon the earth, and to rule over the day and over the night, and to cause to divide the light from the darkness. And the Gods watched those things which they had ordered until they obeyed. (Abraham 4:1–18)

What exactly can we learn from these three accounts? It appears that our Heavenly Father, along with other members of the Godhead, authorized the creation of this earth on which we live. From the Apostle John we know that the premortal Jesus Christ was given the assignment to actually create the earth:

> In the beginning was the Word, and the Word was with God, and the Word was God. The same was in the beginning with God.
>
> All things were made by him; and without him was not any thing made that was made. In him was life; and the life was the light of men.
>
> And the light shineth in darkness; and the darkness comprehended it not. . . .
>
> He was in the world, and the world was made by him, and the world knew him not. He came unto his own, and his own received him not.
>
> But as many as received him, to them gave he power to become the sons of God, even to them that believe on his name. . . .
>
> And the Word was made flesh, and dwelt among us, (and we beheld his glory, the glory as of the only begotten of the Father,) full of grace and truth.
>
> John bare witness of him, and cried, saying, This was he of whom I spake, He that cometh after me is preferred before me: for he was before me.
>
> And of his fulness have all we received, and grace for grace. For the law was given by Moses, but grace and truth came by Jesus Christ. (John 1:1–5, 10–12, 14–17)

The elements that compose the earth are eternal in nature, and they were organized to form this earth. The actual work of forming the earth was completed in six "days," with the seventh "day" being one of rest from those labors.

Three main theories exist on just what constituted a "day": (1) a day according to man's reckoning, or a twenty-four-hour period; (2) a day according to our Heavenly Father's reckoning, or one thousand of our years; or (3) an era or a period of time, such as "The day of the knights of the round table," and so forth. Abraham tells us:

> And I, Abraham, had the Urim and Thummim, which the Lord my God had given unto me, in Ur of the Chaldees;
>
> And I saw the stars, that they were very great, and that one of them was nearest unto the throne of God; and there were many great ones which were near unto it;
>
> And the Lord said unto me: These are the governing ones; and the name of the great one is Kolob, because it is near unto me, for I am the Lord thy God: I have set this one to govern all those which belong to the same order as that upon which thou standest.
>
> And the Lord said unto me, by the Urim and Thummim, that Kolob was after the manner of the Lord, according to its times and seasons in the revolutions thereof; that one revolution was a day unto the Lord, after his manner of reckoning, it being one thousand years according to the time appointed unto that whereon thou standest. This is the reckoning of the Lord's time, according to the reckoning of Kolob. (Abraham 3:1–4)
>
> And the Gods commanded the man, saying: Of every tree of the garden thou mayest freely eat, but of the tree of knowledge of good and evil, thou shalt not eat of it; for in the time that thou eatest thereof, thou shalt surely die. Now I, Abraham, saw that it was after the Lord's time, which was after the time of Kolob; for as yet the Gods had not appointed unto Adam his reckoning." (Abraham 5:12–13)

Whatever theory we subscribe to, one thing should be clear. This earth, the animals thereon, and mankind were not just a fly-by-night happenstance. If you believe in the scriptures, the ancestors of man certainly didn't slither out of some swamp and then eventually evolve into an advanced state, carrying around big clubs and dragging women around by their hair. To subscribe to that theory would most surely make the scriptural accounts null and void. Rather, the Creation was a well-postulated, intricate plan that didn't just happen!

In Genesis we read that the Lord planted every plant and tree and caused them to grow for the benefit of mankind (Genesis 2:9). Moses gives us further insight into the Creation:

> And every plant of the field before it was in the earth, and every herb of the field before it grew. For I, the Lord God, created all things, of which I have spoken, spiritually, before they were naturally upon the face of the earth. For I, the Lord God, had not caused it to rain upon the face of the earth. And I, the Lord God, had created all the children of men; and not yet a man to till the ground; for in heaven created I them; and there was not yet flesh upon the earth, neither in the water, neither in the air. . . .
>
> And I, the Lord God, planted a garden eastward in Eden, and there I put the man whom I had formed.
>
> And out of the ground made I, the Lord God, to grow every tree, naturally, that is pleasant to the sight of man; and man could behold it. And it became also a living soul. For it was spiritual in the day that I created it; for it remaineth in the sphere in which I, God, created it, yea, even all things which I prepared for the use of man; and man saw that it was good for food. And I, the Lord God, planted the tree of life also in the midst of the garden, and also the tree of knowledge of good and evil. (Moses 3:5, 8–9)

It appears that the account from the book of Abraham is referring mostly to the spiritual creation, where the "Gods" counseled before the actual physical creation of the earth (Abraham 5, chapter heading), whereas the book of Moses mentions that creation (as cited above) but focuses mainly on the actual physical creation. These two additional resources give us valuable insights not found in the Genesis account.

From these three accounts we see that the Father of heaven and earth organized the Creation and then commissioned its fulfillment through the holy priesthood. The Creation was so well planned that everything that was created physically was first created spiritually. The creation of this earth and all of its inhabitants was part of the grand plan of our Heavenly Father, set in motion to facilitate His work and glory (Moses 1:39).

Chapter 3

The Fall of Man: Curse or Blessing?

And in that day the Holy Ghost fell upon Adam, which beareth record of the Father and the Son, saying: I am the Only Begotten of the Father from the beginning, henceforth and forever, that as thou hast fallen thou mayest be redeemed, and all mankind, even as many as will.

And in that day Adam blessed God and was filled, and began to prophesy concerning all the families of the earth, saying: Blessed be the name of God, for because of my transgression my eyes are opened, and in this life I shall have joy, and again in the flesh I shall see God.

And Eve, his wife, heard all these things and was glad, saying: Were it not for our transgression we never should have had seed, and never should have known good and evil, and the joy of our redemption, and the eternal life which God giveth unto all the obedient.

And Adam and Eve blessed the name of God, and they made all things known unto their sons and their daughters.

—Moses 5:9–12

Throughout the annals of time, whenever our Heavenly Father has desired to communicate with his children on the earth, He has chosen to do so through a living prophet (Amos 3:7). These chosen mouthpieces were called and ordained to receive His words so that mankind would know what He would have them know, do, and become. The first of these patriarchs was our father Adam, who, along with his wife Eve, were selected before the world was, to be our first parents. Upon their heads was placed the responsibility of guiding the destiny of the entire human family.

The account in Genesis informs us that our Father in Heaven placed them in the Garden of Eden in what might appear to be a no-win situation. They were commanded first and foremost to multiply and replenish the earth (Genesis 1:28). They were also told not to partake of the fruit of the tree of knowledge of good and evil (Genesis 2:9, 15–17). On the surface this appears to make little sense. From the writings of Moses, however, we get additional, insightful dialogue that allows us to see our Father's intentions:

"But of the tree of the knowledge of good and evil, thou shalt not eat of it, nevertheless, thou mayest choose for thyself, for it is given unto thee; but, remember that I forbid it, for in the day thou eatest thereof thou shalt surely die" (Moses 3:17).

Why would our Father in Heaven give our first parents two commands that seem to contradict each other? To answer that question, we must understand a few other things. For true agency to be in force, alternative choices must exist, and we must understand the blessings and consequences that will accompany those choices. Knowledge is essential for us to act willfully and not ignorantly. Only when these conditions exist can we truly be responsible for our own destiny. It wouldn't be equitable if we were to be held accountable for something that we had no way of knowing.

When we know both sides of a choice, the positive and the negative, we have nobody to blame for our individual situations but ourselves. As mentioned in chapter one, the Father works in light, not in darkness. In like manner, He will never destroy a people on the earth until they have been sufficiently warned and given a chance to repent and change. Without a knowledge of the results of our choices, it is impossible to truly commit sin. Again, sin is defined as willfully going against good after having an understanding of it (James 4:17). With this understanding, perhaps we can now look somewhat intelligently at the circumstances that deal with the fall of Man.

Adam and Eve were placed in the Garden of Eden in a state of innocence. They were told that they were to multiply and replenish the earth. That might seem to the average individual as a simple task, but if we read the entire story of life in the garden, there appears to be a variable that would make that task impossible. After Eve had succumbed to the temptation of the adversary and partaken of the fruit of the tree of knowledge of good and evil, she gave of the fruit to Adam. Adam was apparently set on keeping the counsel of the Father to abstain from the fruit. But what about the words of the Father:

"And the Lord God said, It is not good that the man should be alone; I will make him an help meet for him" (Genesis 2:18).

Once Eve had partaken of the fruit, her destiny was set, and it stands to reason that Adam probably followed suit, partaking so as not to be left alone. It was in the partaking that we find a key to understanding what separates Latter-day Saint beliefs from those of the rest of Christianity:

> And the woman said unto the serpent, We may eat of the fruit of the trees of the garden: But of the fruit of the tree which is in the midst of the garden, God hath said, ye shall not eat of it, neither shall ye touch it, lest ye die.
>
> And the serpent said unto the woman, Ye shall not surely die: for God doth know that in the day ye eat thereof, then your eyes shall be opened, and ye shall be as the gods, knowing good and evil.
>
> And when the woman saw that the tree was good for food, and that it was pleasant to the eyes, and a tree to be desired to make one wise, she took of the fruit thereof, and did eat, and gave also unto her husband her; and he did eat.
>
> And the eyes of them both were opened, and they knew that they were naked. (Genesis 3:2–7)

It wasn't possible for Adam and Eve to sin to the degree for which most of Christianity condemns them. They didn't have the knowledge of good and evil required, according to the Bible, to commit sin of significant magnitude (remember James 4:17) until after they had partaken of the fruit. The tree was "of knowledge of good and evil" (Moses 3:9), and although they may have been counseled not to do something, that didn't necessarily constitute an understanding of the blessings or consequences attached to that directive.

Adam and Eve were told that in the day they ate of the fruit of that particular tree, they would surely die. In other words, while they were in the garden they were living a terrestrial existence as immortal beings, incapable of physical death. In the day they ate of the fruit, however, they would be cast out of the garden. They would become mortal beings, subject to physical death, and be forced to make their way in a telestial world, fraught with sin and suffering. As Satan often does, he used a number of truths and then slipped in a lie, making the whole thing a lie. Yes, they would become as the gods, knowing good from evil, but die they most assuredly would.

Another fact still needs to be addressed: the command they had been given to multiply and replenish the earth. It would be quite impossible for a man and a woman to be partners in the procreation process without knowledge of what it means to be "naked." No, it doesn't appear that Adam and Eve had sufficient knowledge to have committed the horrible sin of which most of Christianity accuses them. And if indeed they did not sin, then it would stand to reason that none of the rest of us would have their sin upon our heads at our mortal birth—a fact that would rule out the need for infant baptism as well.

Children are the most pure of all beings on the earth. If that were not the case, the Savior surely would not have taught that unless we became like little children, we would never see the kingdom (Matthew 18:3).

It was our Father in Heaven's desire that Adam and Eve make precisely the decision they made. If they hadn't, His plan would have come to naught. None of us would have been able to come to earth and gain physical bodies or undergo the experiences that our Father desired for us to gain through the facilitation of that plan. The fact that He foreordained a Savior to redeem us would seem to be evidence of His foreknowledge of the transgression of Adam and Eve.

The Bible is relatively silent concerning the aftermath of the Fall in the Garden of Eden. We are fortunate, however, to have additional scripture concerning this critical event:

> And after Adam and Eve had partaken of the forbidden fruit they were driven out of the garden of Eden, to till the earth. And they have brought forth children; yea, even the family of all the earth.
>
> And the days of the children of men were prolonged, according to the will of God, that they might repent while in the flesh; wherefore, their state became a state of probation, and their time was lengthened, according to the commandments which the Lord God gave unto the children of men. For he gave commandment that all men must repent; for he showed unto all men that they were lost, because of the transgression of their parents.
>
> And now, behold, if Adam had not transgressed he would not have fallen, but he would have remained in the garden of Eden. And all things which were created must have remained in the same state in which they were after they were created; and they must have remained forever, and had no end.
>
> And they would have had no children; wherefore they would have remained in a state of innocence, having no joy, for they knew no misery; doing no good, for they knew no sin.
>
> But behold, all things have been done in the wisdom of him who knoweth all things. Adam fell that men might be; and men are, that they might have joy.
>
> And the Messiah cometh in the fulness of time, that he may redeem the children of men from the fall. And because that they are redeemed from

> the fall they have become free forever, knowing good from evil; to act for themselves and not to be acted upon, save it be by the punishment of the law at the great and last day, according to the commandments which God hath given. (2 Nephi 2:19–26)

> And in that day the Holy Ghost fell upon Adam, which beareth record of the Father and the Son, saying: I am the Only Begotten of the Father from the beginning, henceforth and forever, that as thou hast fallen thou mayest be redeemed, and all mankind, even as many as will.
>
> And in that day Adam blessed God and was filled, and began to prophesy concerning all the families of the earth, saying: Blessed be the name of God, for because of my transgression my eyes are opened, and in this life I shall have joy, and again in the flesh I shall see God.
>
> And Eve, his wife, heard all these things and was glad, saying: Were it not for our transgression we never should have had seed, and never should have known good and evil, and the joy of our redemption, and the eternal life which God giveth unto all the obedient.
>
> And Adam and Eve blessed the name of God, and they made all things known unto their sons and their daughters. (Moses 5:9–12)

This additional information gives us insight into the feelings of our first parents after their fall. It indicates that they viewed that fall as a fall forward, not backward. This added information changes everything that the majority of Christianity believes concerning the state in which we are all born into mortality. Rather than coming here born with the "sin of Adam" upon our heads, we come here without spot or sin. Therefore we do not need baptism until we become accountable for our sin.

Anyone who has witnessed the birth and growth of children will recognize that it is the condition of the world that they are born into that acts upon them and entices them to sin, but children don't come here predisposed to break the commandments of God. Each of us comes here pure from the presence of our Father in Heaven. Thus we should look at our first parents with gratitude rather than with contempt. Without their fall, none of us would be here in mortality, but thanks to them, we all got our chance to progress to this, our second estate.

Chapter 4

The Atonement of Jesus Christ

For behold, I, God, have suffered these things for all, that they might not suffer if they would repent; but if they would not repent they must suffer even as I; which suffering caused myself, even God, the greatest of all, to tremble because of pain, and to bleed at every pore, and to suffer both body and spirit—and would that I might not drink the bitter cup, and shrink—nevertheless, glory be to the Father, and I partook and finished my preparations unto the children of men.

—D&C 19:16–19

No single event in the history of the universe equals in importance the atonement of Jesus Christ. After the fall of man in the Garden of Eden, sin came into the world. Each of us in turn would come to earth for our mortal experience. We would be born into a world subject to sin and its inherent pitfalls. There is a law irrevocably decreed in heaven that prohibits one who is guilty of willful sin from living in the Father's presence. Each of us at some point will be guilty of sin to some degree (1 John 1:8). It would therefore stand to reason that none of us would be allowed to return to live with our Father in Heaven because we were all unclean. If that remained the case, the grand plan of the Father would be frustrated.

As mentioned in chapter one, there was a way that provided for each of us to be able to experience the foibles of mortality without damning ourselves from our eternal progression. It would require that someone who was without sin pay the ransom for us—a ransom we were incapable of paying ourselves.

It is impossible for us to truly repent of willful sin without suffering for disobedience. The greater the magnitude of the sin, the more intensely we must suffer to be forgiven for that impropriety. President Spencer W. Kimball, a modern-day prophet, has commented on this doctrine:

> One has not begun to repent until he has suffered intensely for his sins. . . . If a person hasn't suffered, he hasn't repented. . . . He has got to go through a change in his system whereby he suffers and then forgiveness is a possibility. . . .
>
> Very frequently people think they have repented and are worthy of forgiveness when all they have done is to express sorrow or regret at the unfortunate happening. (*Teachings of Spencer W. Kimball,* 87–99)

Can you understand why the belief that we need merely profess faith in order to qualify for salvation is so glaringly insufficient? How could we possibly think that forgiveness for willful sin on our part would require so little when the price those sins exacted upon the Savior was so excruciatingly great? To merely profess our faith and then expect Him to just make everything "all right" through His suffering appears so superficial, so absolutely token-like in nature!

Have you ever wondered what it would take for a person to literally sweat drops of blood from every pore? I have pondered on that many times, and I would like to share an insight that I received from the Holy Ghost on one sacred occasion.

One day, early in my teaching career, I was attempting to teach the Atonement to one of my seminary classes. I was about to say that it is impossible for us to understand what it was like for the Savior to take upon Himself the suffering for all of the sins of mankind. As I began to speak, the Spirit enlightened my mind and heart to the point that I believe I was able to gain a glimpse, albeit a small one, of just what it was that caused Him, the greatest of all, "to tremble because of pain, and to bleed at every pore, and to suffer both body and spirit—and would that I might not drink the bitter cup, and shrink" (D&C 19:18).

Reflect for a moment on your life. I don't wish for anyone to dredge up the harrowing memories of their past life, but for the sake of understanding, think back on your life to a trying experience. Perhaps it was when you committed a sin that caused you to suffer greatly. Perhaps it was when you were depressed because of a death or some other tragedy. Whatever our situation, I'm sure that each of us has experienced extreme anguish.

What struck me so profoundly that day and on many occasions since is this: If I were to take all of the times that I have been, or ever will be, depressed or harrowed up with pain, both in body and spirit, and combine that with the pain, suffering, and anguish of every other person who would ever be born on this earth, and put them all on the shoulders of one man at one time, and ask him to bear them by himself, I wonder what that would feel like?

That is a horrifying thought, but that, in essence, is what the Savior endured when He suffered and bled from every pore in the Garden of Gethsemane. That's apparently what our Savior went through for each of us so that we wouldn't have to, if we would just repent (D&C 19:16–17). Therefore, if you or I can't quite get the picture of all of this, if it somehow just doesn't strike us as reality, then I have one more sobering thought for us to ponder. It comes from the Savior's words as found in scripture: "But if they would not repent they must suffer even as I" (D&C 19:17).

Ponder the words of President Spencer W. Kimball concerning this principle of the gospel:

> Many do not learn that cost in this life, simply because the payments may be deferred. What effect would it have if the payments were always "in cash"? A thoughtful comment whose authorship I do not know considers that point:
>
> "I am convinced that if each thing we did wrong had a price tag on it, the world would experience a phenomenal change. That is to say, if we could see what each such wrongdoing is costing, we might think twice before committing the act. Unfortunately, we often have only a vague notion of the terrible cost or allow Satan to sugar-coat our concept of circumstances. But, let us stop and look at some of these prices. It is quite certain that if all rewards for goodness were immediately available and all the penalties for evil were immediately assessed and suffered there would seldom be a second evil—but then, that would tamper with one's precious free agency."
>
> We might add that one's position makes no difference to the inescapability of the consequences of sin. In the Church, the bishop, the stake president, the apostle—all are subject to the same laws of right living, and penalties follow their sins just as for the other members of the Church. None are exempt from the results of sin, as regards either Church action against the offender or the effects of sin upon the soul. (*Miracle of Forgiveness,* 144–45).

I don't know how these words ring in your ears, but in mine they sound like this: "If you don't understand what He went through for you, just choose not to repent, and you'll find out firsthand what it was like." Here's a quote from one of the finest talks ever delivered on repentance:

> Am I suggesting that the benefits of the Atonement are not available for the person who heedlessly sins? Of course not. But I am suggesting that there is a relationship between sin and suffering that is not understood by people who knowingly sin in the expectation that all the burden of suffering will be borne by Another, that the sin is all theirs but that the suffering is all His. That is not the way. Repentance, which is an assured passage to an eternal destination, is nevertheless not a free ride. (Dallin H. Oaks, "Sin and Suffering," *Ensign,* July 1992, 71–72)

This principle is also taught to us plainly in the New Testament:

> That which we have seen and heard declare we unto you, that ye also may have fellowship with us: and truly our fellowship is with the Father, and with his Son Jesus Christ.
>
> And these things write we unto you, that your joy may be full. This then is the message which we have heard of him, and declare unto you, that God is light, and in him is no darkness at all.
>
> If we say that we have fellowship with him, and walk in darkness, we lie, and do not the truth:
>
> But if we walk in the light, as he is in the light, we have fellowship one with another, and the blood of Jesus Christ his Son cleanseth us from all sin. (1 John 1:3–7)

It is evident from the last verse that certain conditions must be met if we are to have full access to the benefits of the Savior's atonement. Modern scripture would seem to verify that doctrine:

> For all who will have a blessing at my hands

> shall abide the law which was appointed for that blessing, and the conditions thereof, as were instituted from before the foundation of the world. (D&C 132:5)

> There is a law, irrevocably decreed in heaven before the foundations of this world, upon which all blessings are predicated—and when we obtain any blessing from God, it is by obedience to that law upon which it is predicated. (D&C 130:20–21)

Elder Theodore M. Burton said:

> Repentance is a mechanism for personal growth and development. . . . Suffering is not repentance. Suffering comes from *lack* of complete repentance. . . . Punishment is not repentance. Punishment *follows* disobedience and *precedes* repentance. . . .
>
> Remorse is not repentance. Remorse and sorrow continue because a person has *not* yet fully repented. . . .
>
> The meaning of repentance is not that people be punished, but rather that they change their lives so that God can help them escape eternal punishment and enter into his rest with joy and rejoicing. If we have this understanding, our anxiety and fears will be relieved. *Repentance* will become a welcome and treasured word in our religious vocabulary. ("The Meaning of Repentance," *Ensign,* August 1988, 7–8)

Here we can see that our Savior's main concern is that we become as He is. He is concerned about us and about our eternal welfare.

Over the years, as I have studied and pondered upon the Atonement, I have concluded that there was a lot more to this selfless sacrifice than meets the eye. For instance, in the account given us in the book of Luke, we discover that the Savior had to face this ultimate test of courage on His own, without help from His Father.

Though we learn that in the Garden of Gethsemane the Father sent His support—"And there appeared an angel unto him from heaven, strengthening him" (Luke 22:43)—it was nevertheless requisite that the Savior of mankind pay the price of all sin on His own: "And being in an agony he prayed more earnestly: and his sweat was as it were great drops of blood falling down to the ground" (Luke 22:44).

It also appears that the horror that He experienced that night in the garden and the next day on the cross was caused by the buffetings of Satan and his evil legions of followers. All of this He suffered without the aid of the Holy Ghost to strengthen Him against the blows of the evil one and his emissaries.

In some way, very real yet incomprehensible to the human mind, He faced the buffetings of Satan—no doubt inflicted by him and all of his emissaries—and survived. He took everything that the adversary had to dish out and came off conqueror. At one point, on the cross, He was offered vinegar and gall, a mercy drink, to help deaden the excruciating pain, but He refused it and finished His preparations to the Father. He had to endure all of the suffering without a respite from the pain, a requirement if this offering of grace were to be acceptable to atone for the sins of the entire human race.

The horror He was subject to earlier in the Garden of Gethsemane apparently returned as He hung on the cross at Golgotha. This was Satan's one last shot at trying to destroy the plan of the Father through the Redeemer, the key to the entire plan. This is evidenced by the words Jesus uttered in horrible agony: "My God, my God, why hast thou forsaken me?" (Matthew 27:46).

I am not implying that any of us is capable of comprehending the extent of the Savior's suffering. To the contrary, I am certain that it is not possible for any mortal to do so. Yet his incomprehensible suffering is what paid the price for our sins. He trod the winepress alone, and when He was sure that His sacrifice was sufficient, He reported to His Father that it was done and voluntarily let His spirit slip into the world of spirits (John 19:30; Luke 23:46).

Now I wish to quote the words of a modern-day apostle, Elder Melvin

J. Ballard, concerning the Father's love for us and the Savior's finishing of the Atonement:

> It was to make you feel what our Father felt, when He who loved His Son better than it is possible for mortals to love their own flesh and blood, gave His Son to the world, for the world's redemption, for the world's peace, and the world's salvation. Do you not think that while the Father, who had the power to save His Son from the abuse, from the crown of thorns, from the whippings and mistreatment, do you not think it was a trial for Him, who had the power to save His Son, to stand by and witness the appeal of the Son, in agony, until great drops of blood came from His body. "If it is possible, save me, O Father!
>
> Think of your own child. If your child was in distress, is there a man among us entrusted with the power to save, and would not use it? God knows that we are so human that if He should give us power to save our own, we would save them every time. And yet he had the power to save and did not save. What mother would not fly through fire and water at hearing the appeal of her child in distress? How it must have tried the Father to hear the cry and lamentation of the Son: "If it is possible, Father, let it pass by!"
>
> I say the Father was grief-stricken when He heard the taunting of those who stood by? "He saved others, why doesn't He save Himself?" After the hours of grief and agony, there came a moment when Jesus cried out, "My God, my God, why hast thou forsaken me?"
>
> If Jesus truly said that, it was not that the Father had forsaken, but that the hour had arrived, which often arrives in our own human experience, an hour when the mother, for example, who

> cannot any longer stand to bear the sight of her dying child, after the farewell is given, is taken out of the room, not to witness the last dying struggles of her loved one.
>
> And so, the Father, taxed to the utmost, had withdrawn, and somewhere was weeping for His beloved Son. Even He could not stand the sight any longer. But as I have thought of it, in my heart I have thanked Him, that when in that critical moment, He might have saved His Son, He saw us, perishing in the grave, lost to Him, and lost to that salvation which is to come. He saw that on the one hand, and the appeals and the suffering of His Son on the other, and He decided in our favor, and allowed the suffering and death of His Son. And in that, I maintain that He has manifested His love for us.
>
> That ought to make us trust him, though clouds may gather and darkness come, though like Job of old, "He may slay me, yet shall I trust Him." Because I know that He loves me, and I know that He is not anxious to see my tears of sorrow and distress. I know that He designs to purge me and purify me, and that behind this apparent darkness and cloud, there is a smiling face. (in Conference Report, October 1914, 68–69)

Consider also the words of a leading Brigham Young University professor on the topic of the Father's sacrifice of His Son:

> "Yet it pleased the Lord to bruise him" (Isaiah 53:10; Mosiah 14:10). This is a verse that requires careful consideration. God our Eternal Father loved his Only Begotten and, like any parent, surely anguished with the pain of his child. And yet, as infinitely painful as it must have been for Elohim, the hours of agony were

> necessary—they were a part of that plan of the Father of which Jehovah had been the chief advocate and proponent in premortality. Indeed it was needful that the "Lamb slain from the foundation of the world" be slain, in order that life and immortality might be brought to light. And thus "it pleased the Lord [the Father] to bruise him," in the sense that Jesus carried out to the fullest the will of the Father, in spite of the pain associated with the implementation of the terms and conditions of that will.
>
> "Oh," Elder Melvin J. Ballard said, "in that moment when He might have saved His Son, I thank Him and praise Him that He did not fail us, for He had not only the love of His Son in mind, but He also had love for us. I rejoice that He did not interfere, and that His love for us made it possible for Him to endure to look upon the sufferings of His Son and give Him finally to us, our Savior and our Redeemer.
>
> Without Him, without His sacrifice, we would have remained, and would never have come glorified into His presence. And so this is what it cost, in part, for our Father in heaven to give the gift of His Son unto men." (Robert L. Millet, *Power of the Word,* [Salt Lake City: Deseret Book, 1991], 119)

In light of this information, it would seem to be inexcusable for any of us even to entertain the thought of committing sin with the attitude that we can always "just repent later." Yet there are many today who have precisely that mindset. Frequently over the years, I have heard of various people who have committed what I would term "premeditated" serious sin, with the intention of just repenting later and being "good as new."

Somehow, I feel that it won't be quite as easy to repent for such an offense as it would be if they had fallen unintentionally. Repentance is a gift of inestimable value, and it is most assuredly there for each of us when we need it. Nevertheless, it should be obvious for us to recognize that it is far better when we abstain from sin as much as possible so that our need of that gift is minimized.

Truly it seems wiser to follow the old adage "It is better to prepare and prevent than to repair and repent."

Chapter 5

Obedience, the First Law of Heaven

There is a law, irrevocably decreed in heaven before the foundations of this world, upon which all blessings are predicated—and when we obtain any blessing from God, it is by obedience to that law upon which it is predicated.

—D&C 130:20–21

Some decades ago Elder S. Dilworth Young delivered an address that I have never forgotten concerning the principle of obedience. He said:

> Many years ago President Charles W. Penrose of the First Presidency attended a sacrament meeting in Richards Ward in Salt Lake City. Just before the meeting commenced President Penrose walked down the aisle toward the pulpit, accompanied by the bishop. About halfway down he stopped, turned to the bishop, and inquired of him, "who put that sign there?" "That sign" was a placard that was attached to the front of the pulpit and that read: "Order is the first law of heaven."
>
> The bishop didn't know but supposed that the sign had been installed by one of the auxiliaries. Nothing more was said. The march down the aisle continued, and the meeting duly commenced.
>
> I do not know what subject President Penrose intended to speak on when he arrived at the chapel, but when he arose to speak, he said that order is not the first law of heaven, but that obedience is. He spent the next 45 minutes marshalling instances and scripture to prove his thesis. The main point that impressed me, a boy at the time, was that by obedience order may be established and that without obedience there will be no order, but chaos . . .
>
> We have learned that in order to obey the Lord we must obey his servants. Each presiding officer is to be obeyed in righteousness, in the field of his presidency. And so it is clear that we obey the President of the Church, the president of the stake, the bishop of the ward, and the president of the quorum, each in his field of service.

> And finally, forgotten by many as a requirement of heaven, is the necessity of obedience to our parents. . . .
>
> Let children learn this law of God as a commandment to be obeyed. Let us also teach them that this is the great restoration of the gospel promised by ancient prophets. Let us teach them that obedience to their parents, and to those who preside over them, from the quorum leader to the president of Church, is the foundation of their future success in this world and their exaltation in the world to come. (Young, "Obedience—the First Law of Heaven," *Improvement Era,* December 1966, 1108–9)

President Joseph F. Smith had this to say:

> Christ is responsible for the man so far as the man walks in obedience to the laws and commandments he has given, but no further, and so far will his atoning blood redeem and cleanse from sin; so far as they obey them will the principles of eternal life revealed in the Gospel have effect upon the souls of men, so also with women. (in *Journal of Discourses,* 16:247)

The lack of obedience was the principal cause of all the trouble experienced by the Father's spirit family in the pre-earthly war in heaven. Lucifer's lack of obedience to our Father's plan is what got him, along with his followers, banished from God's presence (Isaiah 14:12–16; Revelation 12:7–9). Yes, it would appear that obedience was indeed the first law of heaven, and it also appears that the children of the God of Heaven have struggled with that principle since before they came to earth for their mortal experience.

When Adam and Eve were banished from the Garden of Eden, they were instructed to obey certain rites as outlined by our Father:

> And Adam and Eve, his wife, called upon the name of the Lord, and they heard the voice of the Lord from the way toward the Garden of Eden, speaking unto them, and they saw him not; for they were shut out from his presence.
>
> And he gave unto them commandments, that they should worship the Lord their God, and should offer the firstlings of their flocks, for an offering unto the Lord. And Adam was obedient unto the commandments of the Lord.
>
> And after many days an angel of the Lord appeared unto Adam, saying: Why dost thou offer sacrifices unto the Lord? And Adam said unto him: I know not, save the Lord commanded me. (Moses 5:4–6)

What an outstanding example of obedience! Adam didn't know why, but he didn't question it; he just obeyed. Another great example of the principle of obedience comes to us from the Book of Mormon:

> Nevertheless, I have received a commandment of the Lord that I should make these plates, for the special purpose that there should be an account engraven of the ministry of my people.
>
> Upon the other plates should be engraven an account of the reign of the kings, and the wars and contentions of my people; wherefore these plates are for the more part of the ministry; and the other plates are for the more part of the reign of the kings and the wars and contentions of my people.
>
> Wherefore, the Lord hath commanded me to make these plates for a wise purpose in him, which purpose I know not.
>
> But the Lord knoweth all things from the beginning; wherefore, he prepareth a way to accomplish all his works among the children of men; for behold, he hath all power unto the

> fulfilling of all his words. And thus it is. Amen. (1 Nephi 9:3–6)

Some would point fingers at such acts of obedience as being "blind faith." But I submit that precisely the opposite it true. It is an abundance of faith, not a lack of it that causes people to act when they don't fully understand the reasons behind the command. That faith tells them, just as it did Nephi, that somehow, someway, things will work out for their good if they will do what the Savior asks. When they believe totally in the person giving the command, their faith allows them to go beyond the light into the dark, believing that He will not lead them into danger. In fact, it appears that it is our unquestioning obedience that is the vehicle by which our faith can grow:

> And now, I, Moroni, would speak somewhat concerning these things; I would show unto the world that faith is things which are hoped for and not seen; wherefore, dispute not because ye see not, for ye receive no witness until after the trial of your faith.
>
> For it was by faith that Christ showed himself unto our fathers, after he had risen from the dead; and he showed not himself unto them until after they had faith in him; wherefore, it must needs be that some had faith in him, for he showed himself not unto the world.
>
> But because of the faith of men he has shown himself unto the world, and glorified the name of the Father, and prepared a way that thereby others might be partakers of the heavenly gift, that they might hope for those things which they have not seen.
>
> Wherefore, ye may also have hope, and be partakers of the gift, if ye will but have faith. Behold it was by faith that they of old were called after the holy order of God. (Ether 12:6–10)

True, unquestioning obedience is not always easy to attain but is necessary nonetheless if we are to strive to become as the Savior is, as the words of a modern prophet bear out:

> This brings us to the supreme test. Are we willing to become totally obedient to God's law, relinquishing our own wills and desires in the process? There comes a time in our lives when a definite decision must be made. Obedience is not tested when life is calm and pleasant and when we are deriving spiritual satisfaction from doing good; but when thoughts or pressures persuade us to act in a way contrary to God's commandments, then obedience is put to the test. (Howard Hunter, *Teachings of Howard W. Hunter,* 24)

The supreme test we will each face in this life is our willingness to be totally obedient when we don't necessarily want to be. It appears that the level of our obedience is probably the best way to truly measure the depth of our faith.

A story from the Old Testament always comes to mind whenever the principle of obedience arises. It is found in 1 Samuel and involves Israel's first king, a man named Saul. Saul was a mighty man who had earned the respect and admiration of Israel through his obedience to the things of God. He was a man of great physical prowess and stood a head taller than anyone else in the camp of Israel. For that reason the people desired that he become their king and lead them against their enemies. They were counseled by the prophet Samuel against having a king but failed to listen to his prophetic words that a king would lead them into sin and bondage.

The Lord relented to their request, and Samuel crowned Saul as Israel's first king. He did all right at first, but eventually he, like most kings, began to think that his position was bigger than the laws of God. The people were preparing to go into battle, and Saul was waiting for Samuel to come and offer a sacrifice before they embarked. He became impatient and decided to go ahead and offer the sacrifice himself. Anyone who understands the law of Moses knows that only holders of the holy priesthood could offer sacrifice, but Saul's large opinion of himself got in the way of his obedience, and he offered the sacrifice before Samuel arrived.

Let's pick up the story from there:

> Then came the word of the Lord unto Samuel, saying, It repenteth me that I have set up Saul to be king: for he is turned back from following me, and hath not performed my commandments. And it grieved Samuel; and he cried unto the Lord all night.
>
> And when Samuel rose early to meet Saul in the morning, it was told Samuel, saying, Saul came to Carmel, and, behold, he set him up a place, and is gone about, and passed on, and gone down to Gilgal.
>
> And Samuel came to Saul: and Saul said unto him, Blessed be thou of the Lord: I have performed the commandment of the Lord.
>
> And Samuel said, What meaneth then this bleating of the sheep in mine ears, and the lowing of the oxen which I hear?
>
> And Saul said, They have brought them from the Amalekites: for the people spared the best of the sheep and of the oxen, to sacrifice unto the Lord thy God; and the rest we have utterly destroyed.
>
> Then Samuel said unto Saul, Stay, and I will tell thee what the Lord hath said to me this night. And he said unto him, Say on.
>
> And Samuel said, When thou wast little in thine own sight, wast thou not made the head of the tribes of Israel, and the Lord anointed thee king over Israel?
>
> And the Lord sent thee on a journey, and said, Go and utterly destroy the sinners the Amalekites, and fight against them until they be consumed.
>
> Wherefore then didst thou not obey the voice

> of the Lord, but didst fly upon the spoil, and didst evil in the sight of the Lord?
>
> And Saul said unto Samuel, Yea, I have obeyed the voice of the Lord, and have gone the way which the Lord sent me, and have brought Agag the king of Amalek, and have utterly destroyed the Amalekites.
>
> But the people took of the spoil, sheep and oxen, the chief of the things which should have been utterly destroyed, to sacrifice unto the Lord thy God in Gilgal.
>
> And Samuel said, Hath the Lord as great delight in burnt offerings and sacrifices, as in obeying the voice of the Lord? Behold, to obey is better than sacrifice, and to hearken than the fat of rams.
>
> For rebellion is as the sin of witchcraft, and stubbornness is as iniquity and idolatry. Because thou hast rejected the word of the Lord, he hath also rejected thee from being king.
>
> And Saul said unto Samuel, I have sinned: for I have transgressed the commandment of the Lord, and thy words: because I feared the people, and obeyed their voice.
>
> Now therefore, I pray thee, pardon my sin, and turn again with me, that I may worship the Lord.
>
> And Samuel said unto Saul, I will not return with thee: for thou hast rejected the word of the Lord, and the Lord hath rejected thee from being king over Israel. (1 Samuel 15:10–26)

It would appear that had Saul remembered who it was that he had relied upon for his strength and station in Israel, he would have been obedient to the Lord's commands. However, when we mortals begin to think we know more than our God, we seem to somehow fail to feel the need to follow His counsel.

The best example of obedience in all of holy writ comes from the story of the Savior in the Garden of Gethsemane. When faced with the prospect of having to suffer for the sin and anguish of the entire human race, He asked His Father three different times if there might not be an alternative plan? (Matthew 26:39–44). I'm sure that not even Christ had been able to totally envision the extent of the suffering He would have to endure to meet the price of the ransom. The scripture tells us simply:

"And he was withdrawn from them about a stone's cast, and kneeled down, and prayed, saying, Father, if thou be willing, remove this cup from me: nevertheless not my will, but thine, be done" (Luke 22:41–42).

Somehow, the Savior of the universe had mastered Himself to the point that He would do the Father's will at all costs. Because of this victory over self, He has entered into His rest and now desires that each of us have that self-same experience (Matthew 5:48). When we learn to do the things we know we need to do, even when we don't feel like doing them, we will be well on our way to achieving that desire.

Chapter 6

Justification and Sanctification

For by the water ye keep the commandment; by the Spirit ye are justified, and by the blood ye are sanctified.

—Moses 6:60

It is inevitable that each of us will leave this mortal life having become stained by sin. Because of our unclean condition, not one of us will be worthy of being in the presence of our Heavenly Father or our Savior Jesus Christ. Since this is the case, it might appear that the eternal plan of our Father for our salvation is destined for frustration. But our Father's plan is not destined for frustration. The atonement of Jesus Christ allows for all of those who are willing to return to live with the Son and the Father once again. How could our Father in Heaven possibly justify letting us return to His presence when we are all guilty of sin and disobedience at some point in our lives? The answer to that question can be summed up in two simple words: *justification* and *sanctification.* The two laws these two words represent are perhaps not all that simple, but they are definitely a gift of grace from a loving Savior.

Justification in the scriptural sense of the word refers to the process of being pronounced clean and free from sin and guilt. It is simply this: "All covenants, contracts, bonds, obligations, oaths, vows, performances, connections, associations, or expectations (D&C 132:7), in which men must abide to be saved and exalted, must be entered into and performed in righteousness so that the Holy Spirit can justify the candidate for salvation in what has been done" (*Mormon Doctrine,* 408).

Elder Bruce R. McConkie further stated: "Justification is the placing of a divine seal of approval upon the course of conduct pursued by righteous people. It is the approval of the Holy Spirit of the lives being lived by members of the Church. It is a divine ratification of the way of life of the true saints. It is being sealed by the Holy Spirit of Promise" (*New Witness for the Articles of Faith,* 102).

A friend who is an attorney once told me that most cases go to trial not with the intent of finding out whether the person charged with committing the crime actually committed it but rather to find out why the person did it. Determining motivation is critical because it allows the judge or jury to justify whatever sentence they decide to give the accused.

"To be sanctified is to become clean, pure, and spotless; to be free from the blood and sins of the world; to become a new creature of the Holy Ghost, one whose body has been renewed by the rebirth of the Spirit" (McConkie, *Mormon Doctrine,* 675). Sanctification is a state of saintliness, a state attained only by conformity to the laws and ordinances of the gospel. The Father's plan of salvation is the system and means provided whereby men may sanctify their souls and thereby become worthy of a celestial inheritance.

"Sanctification is a basic doctrine of the gospel (D&C 20:31–34). Indeed, the very reason men are commanded to believe, repent, and be baptized is so they 'may be sanctified by the reception of the Holy Ghost' and thereby be enabled to stand spotless before the judgment bar of Christ (2 Nephi 27:19–21)" (*Mormon Doctrine,* 675).

Elder McConkie lends us further insight:

> To be sanctified is to be clean; it is a state of purity and spotlessness in which no taint of sin is found. Only those who die as to sin and are born again to righteousness, becoming thus new creatures of the Holy Ghost, are numbered with the sanctified. In the lives of most of us, sanctification is an ongoing process, and we obtain that glorious status by degrees as we overcome the world and become saints in deed as well as in name. (*New Witness for the Articles of Faith,* 265–66)

Now that we've established definitions for these two laws, let's examine, in layman's terms, what they mean and how they might apply to each of us.

In an attempt to simplify this into terms that all can understand, I will use the Christian world as an example, especially my friends the Baptists. I recently visited one of my high school buddies, who now resides in Texas. During the course of my visit, I was introduced to some of the kindest, friendliest people I have ever met. If ever there were people who embodied the essence of the teachings of Christ concerning the way we treat our fellowmen, it would be these good folk. The Baptist Church not too long ago decided to classify members of my faith as non-Christians. They concluded that since we didn't have the same doctrine concerning the nature of God the Father and His Son, Jesus Christ, we should therefore be delisted from the rolls of Christianity. Apparently, nobody remembered to inform these kind Texans to regard us as heretics.

Another purpose of my trip to Texas was to visit a young man who had been severely burned in an accident. He had received third-degree burns over 97 percent of his body and second-degree burns over the other 3 percent—his head and face. His mother, who is a member of The Church of Jesus Christ of Latter-day Saints, asked me, as a holder of the Melchizedek Priesthood, to give him a priesthood blessing. This young man, who is not a member of the Church, was not expected to live because of the severity of his injuries.

During the course of the week that I was there, my friend and I were invited to eat dinner at the home of one of his friends. As we sat around and chit-chatted, they asked what brought me to Texas. My friend explained that I had come from Utah to give this injured boy a priesthood blessing. The idea of such a thing seemed to them to be a totally normal procedure. I didn't feel ostracized by them in the least. The level of their faith impressed me. The nonchalance in which they took such a sacred and serious undertaking seemed to indicate to me that they assumed that he could be benefited by such an administration on my part. These were not people who considered me an imposter in the Christian world of miracles. The faith these good people demonstrated is something that I have found to be prevalent in the "born-again" culture of the South.

Faith is the first step in our journey to salvation. "But without faith it is impossible to please him: for he that cometh to God must believe that he is, and that he is a rewarder of them that diligently seek him" (Hebrews 11:6).

It is through our faith that we can be justified. Simply put, justification is the process by which we can be allowed to return to the presence of our Father in Heaven, despite the fact that we are less than clean because of our sins. If we truly have faith in Jesus Christ and in His ability to heal us and cleanse us from our sins, and we validate that faith by baptism and other saving ordinances of the holy priesthood, that will justify us being allowed to reenter the presence of them who have no sin. Our faith then would qualify us for that portion of salvation. Those who have not that faith will of necessity be consigned to dwell in another place, "but where God and Christ dwell they cannot come" (D&C 76:112).

Faith alone, however, will not transform us into a person who is one with the Father and the Son (John 17). As explained in chapter four,

Jesus Christ became the person He is by overcoming all of the sin and temptation this mortal world had to offer. Can we possibly think that we can become as He is (Matthew 5:48; 3 Nephi 27:27) by anything less? To subscribe to that belief would appear to me to be nothing short of blasphemy. We have been commanded by our Savior to do our best to strive to become as He is—perfect. That, I would submit, is a pretty tall order! He did not just merely believe; He did! Just as James says, "Faith without works is dead" (James 2:20).

Quite simply, then, by exercising our faith, we believe and are healed, and by our works we become a new person. Perhaps the prophet Mosiah said it best: "[They had] no more disposition to do evil, but to do good continually" (Mosiah 5:2).

Faith is a gift of the Spirit; it is something that our Savior will bestow upon us according to the level of our desire. But being born again in the truest sense is to become changed. It is to become pure. When we have achieved that condition, we will cringe at the very thought of things that are contrary to the teachings and principles of Jesus Christ. Talk is cheap, as the saying goes, but when we are truly born again, that fact will be manifest in our every thought and action. We won't merely talk a good life; we will live the best life we can possibly live. We won't do anything that would bring shame or disappointment to our Savior or our Father in Heaven.

Thus, sanctification is the finisher of our faith. It would appear that it is also a gift of grace that can come only from our Savior, through the Holy Spirit, and only when we have, through our works, conformed our lives to the teachings and principles of the gospel of Jesus Christ. He knows our hearts (D&C 6:16) and has suffered for our iniquities so we would have the opportunity to change our lives to conform to His life. When we have experienced this miraculous change in our nature, we will understand what being "born again" really encompasses.

Justification, it would appear, comes through believing in Jesus Christ, while sanctification is the process of becoming as He is. Either one would be insufficient to save us, in and of itself, without the other. To attain salvation in the ultimate sense, then, we must not only be justified but also become sanctified through the Holy Spirit. I like the analogy offered by a modern-day prophet:

> The Lord works from the inside out. The world works from the outside in. The world would take people out of the slums. Christ takes the slums out of people, and then they take themselves out of the slums. The world would mold men by changing their environment. Christ changes men, who then change their environment. The world would shape human behavior, but Christ can change human nature.
>
> Yes, Christ changes men, and changed men can change the world. Men changed for Christ will be captained by Christ. Finally, men captained by Christ will be consumed in Christ. To paraphrase President Harold B. Lee, they set fire in others because they are on fire (*Stand Ye in Holy Places,* 192).
>
> They do always those things that please the Lord (see John 8:29). Not only would they die for the Lord, but more important, they want to live for Him. (Benson, *The Teachings of Ezra Taft Benson,* 79–80)

When we have reached a condition of being truly sanctified we will be a changed person, one who truly wants to do those things that bring joy and honor to our Heavenly Father and to our Savior. The prophet Mosiah gives us a powerful example of how we will act once we have truly undergone the process of being born again, and how that transformation takes place. As King Benjamin gave his famous sermon to the Nephites, they underwent a marvelous experience:

> And now, it came to pass that when king Benjamin had made an end of speaking the words which had been delivered unto him by the angel of the Lord, that he cast his eyes round about on the multitude, and behold they had fallen to the earth, for the fear of the Lord had come upon them.

And they had viewed themselves in their own carnal state, even less than the dust of the earth. And they all cried aloud with one voice, saying: O have mercy, and apply the atoning blood of Christ that we may receive forgiveness of our sins, and our hearts may be purified; for we believe in Jesus Christ, the Son of God, who created heaven and earth, and all things; who shall come down among the children of men.

And it came to pass that after they had spoken these words the Spirit of the Lord came upon them, and they were filled with joy, having received a remission of their sins, and having peace of conscience, because of the exceeding faith which they had in Jesus Christ who should come, according to the words which king Benjamin had spoken unto them. . . .

And now, it came to pass that when king Benjamin had thus spoken to his people, he sent among them, desiring to know of his people if they believed the words which he had spoken unto them.

And they all cried with one voice, saying: Yea, we believe all the words which thou hast spoken unto us; and also, we know of their surety and truth, because of the Spirit of the Lord Omnipotent, which has wrought a mighty change in us, or in our hearts, that we have no more disposition to do evil, but to do good continually.

And we, ourselves, also, through the infinite goodness of God, and the manifestations of his Spirit, have great views of that which is to come; and were it expedient, we could prophesy of all things.

And it is the faith which we have had on the things which our king has spoken unto us that has brought us to this great knowledge, whereby

> we do rejoice with such exceedingly great joy.
>
> And we are willing to enter into a covenant with our God to do his will, and to be obedient to his commandments in all things that he shall command us, all the remainder of our days, that we may not bring upon ourselves a never-ending torment, as has been spoken by the angel, that we may not drink out of the cup of the wrath of God.
>
> And now, these are the words which king Benjamin desired of them; and therefore he said unto them: Ye have spoken the words that I desired; and the covenant which ye have made is a righteous covenant.
>
> And now, because of the covenant which ye have made ye shall be called the children of Christ, his sons, and his daughters; for behold, this day he hath spiritually begotten you; for ye say that your hearts are changed through faith on his name; therefore, ye are born of him and have become his sons and his daughters.
>
> And under this head ye are made free, and there is no other head whereby ye can be made free. There is no other name given whereby salvation cometh; therefore, I would that ye should take upon you the name of Christ, all you that have entered into the covenant with God that ye should be obedient unto the end of your lives. (Mosiah 4:1–3; 5:1–8)

It would appear, then, that this is the state of persons who have truly been born again. They have no more disposition to do evil but rather to do good continually. President Joseph Fielding Smith stated, "Eternal life is the reward a man shall receive who is obedient to all the laws and covenants of the gospel, and who has, because of his faithfulness, been sanctified through the blood of Jesus Christ. He who receives this great gift shall be like Jesus Christ" (*Doctrines of Salvation,* 2:217).

In conclusion, let me share an explanation that I once heard. I do not know its origin, but I like its premise: "Justice is when you get what you deserve. Mercy is when you don't get what you deserve. Grace is when you get what you don't deserve." Surely we must look to our Savior for extending the latter two to each of us when all we really deserve is the first.

Chapter 7
The History and Destiny of the House of Israel

And it shall come to pass, when thou shalt shew this people all these words, and they shall say unto thee, Wherefore hath the Lord pronounced all this great evil against us? or what is our iniquity? or what is our sin that we have committed against the Lord our God?

Then shalt thou say unto them, Because your fathers have forsaken me, saith the Lord, and have walked after other gods, and have served them, and have worshipped them, and have forsaken me, and have not kept my law; and ye have done worse than your fathers; for, behold, ye walk every one after the imagination of his evil heart, that they may not hearken unto me:

Therefore will I cast you out of this land into a land that ye know not, neither ye nor your fathers; and there shall ye serve other gods day and night; where I will not shew you favour. Therefore, behold, the days come, saith the Lord, that it shall no more be said, The Lord liveth, that brought up the children of Israel out of the land of Egypt;

But, the Lord liveth, that brought up the children of Israel from the land of the north, and from all the lands whither he had driven them: and I will bring them again into their land that I gave unto their fathers. Behold, I will send for many fishers, saith the Lord, and they shall fish them; and after will I send for many hunters, and they shall hunt them from every mountain, and from every hill, and out of the holes of the rocks.

—Jeremiah 16:10–16

In Old Testament times, our Father in Heaven, through His beloved son Jesus Christ, designated and set apart a chosen family. Though we were God's spirit children, we would be required in mortality to align ourselves with that chosen family by becoming Christ's covenant children. All who would come to earth would be required to receive certain saving ordinances through His priesthood at the hands of His authorized servants, who would be of that chosen family. Even if we were not fortunate enough to be born into the lineage of that family, we could nevertheless still have these ordinances bestowed upon us by one of the authorized priesthood holders of that chosen family. In this manner, all of the families of the earth would be blessed (Genesis 12:1–3; 17:1–8).

Though all of the ancient prophets made sacred covenants with God, the first of the great patriarchs to be singled out in this designated lineage was a man named Abraham. The Lord established a special covenant with this great man and bestowed His holy priesthood upon him. Abraham's chosen wife, Sarah, was barren, having been unable to give him offspring. Women in that era looked upon the ability to give their husbands seed, especially sons, as paramount. If a father had no sons to pass on his inheritance to, it would pass to someone else's family.

There was a custom that a woman could give her handmaid (personal servant) to her husband in such cases to raise up seed unto him if she could not do so herself. Whatever the handmaid owned was likewise owned by the wife because she was the wife's property.

"God commanded Abraham, and Sarah gave Hagar to Abraham to wife. And why did she do it? Because this was the law; and from Hagar sprang many people. This, therefore, was fulfilling, among other things, the promises. Was Abraham, therefore, under condemnation? Verily I say unto you, Nay; for I, the Lord, commanded it" (D&C 132:34–35).

Hagar conceived and bore Abraham a son, whom he named Ishmael. It was likewise customary for the eldest son to be what was called the birthright son. This son was to inherit a double portion of the father's property and possessions because it would fall upon his shoulders to take care of his parents in their elderly years. This firstborn son would also be responsible to preside over the family at the father's death.

After thirteen years, Sarah received the blessing of being able to conceive and bear a son in her old age. Her son was named Isaac. After his birth, a great deal of confusion and bad feeling ensued. Sarah was the chosen covenant wife, and therefore it was to her son, Isaac, that the birthright passed. To make sure of that bestowal, Sarah wanted Hagar and Ishmael cast out. It was a difficult decision for Abraham to make, so he consulted God for guidance. Abraham was told to send the two away, that God would provide for and protect them and make from the loins of Ishmael a great nation. Muslims contend that Hagar and Ishmael moved to Mecca and that Abraham continued to keep in contact with them there, a claim that may be true. Nonetheless, both the covenant and the priesthood were passed on to Abraham's son Isaac, who in turn ordained his son Jacob to the holy priesthood. This is clearly stated by the Apostle Paul to the Galatian Saints:

> For it is written, that Abraham had two sons, the one by a bondmaid, the other by a freewoman. But he who was of the bondwoman was born after the flesh; but he of the freewoman was by promise.
>
> Which things are an allegory: for these are the two covenants; the one from the mount Sinai, which gendereth to bondage, which is Agar.
>
> For this Agar is mount Sinai in Arabia, and answereth to Jerusalem which now is, and is in bondage with her children. But Jerusalem which is above is free, which is the mother of us all.
>
> For it is written, Rejoice, thou barren that bearest not; break forth and cry, thou that travailest not: for the desolate hath many more children than she which hath an husband.
>
> Now we, brethren, as Isaac was, are the children of promise. But as then he that was born after the flesh persecuted him that was born after the Spirit, even so it is now. Nevertheless what saith the scripture? Cast out the bondwoman and her son: for the son of the bondwoman shall not be heir with the son of the freewoman.
>
> So then, brethren, we are not children of the bondwoman, but of the free. (Galatians 4:22–31)

Although the seed of Abraham who are not of the lineage of Isaac do not have a literal claim to the blessings established in the covenant that the Lord made with Abraham, they can still become heirs to the spiritual blessings contained in it if they will conform to the process that the Lord set forth (see chapter eight).

The Lord reestablished the Abrahamic covenant with Jacob and gave unto him a new name. His new name was Israel, and he was told that this covenant would be significant to the eternal salvation of the entire human race.

This chosen family would live a checkered existence, one that would see them enslaved for more than four centuries in Egypt, wander in the deserts of Sinai for forty years, become feared conquerors, eventually become the conquered, and then be scattered to the four corners of the earth. Though scattered, Israel was also given the promise that someday the Messiah would be born into the chosen family and that through Christ's atoning sacrifice, they would eventually be extended the opportunity of the gift of eternal redemption. They were also promised that before the second coming of the resurrected Messiah, their seed would be gathered by authority from their lost and fallen state—gathered from the four corners of the earth to which they had been taken.

This gathering must of necessity come at the hands of the tribe of Ephraim. It was to him that the birthright ultimately fell, inasmuch as the tribes were scattered and lost. The prophets of the Old Testament continually prophesied that in the latter days a remnant of the tribe of Ephraim would be raised up to restore the house of Israel to its former station (Deuteronomy 33:13–17). Modern-day prophets likewise have commented on this topic as well. Elder Erastus Snow said the following in Logan, Utah, on May 6, 1882:

> In accordance with the design of the Lord to raise up a peculiar people to himself, a holy nation, a royal Priesthood—a kingdom of Priests, that shall be saviors upon Mount Zion, not only to preach the Gospel to the scattered remnants of Israel, but to save to the uttermost the nations of the Gentiles, inasmuch as they will listen and can be saved by the plan which God has provided.

The first important labor of this ministry is to go abroad and preach the Gospel to the nations. The Gospel of the kingdom must be preached to all people and nations and tongues before the end can come; and by the preaching of the word and the administering of the ordinances of the Gospel, is Israel sought out from among the nations among which they are, especially the seed of unto whom the first promises appertain, the promise of the keys of the Priesthood. For it must be remembered that of all the seed of Abraham whom the Lord chose to bear the keys pertaining to this holy order of Priesthood, the seed of, the son of Joseph, were the first and chief. . . .

Now the same spirit of revelation that sought out the Prophet Joseph from the loins of Joseph who was sold into Egypt, and that raised him up in this dispensation to receive the keys of the Priesthood and to lay the foundation of this great work in the earth, has also called the children of Abraham from among the kingdoms and countries of the earth to first hear and then embrace the everlasting Gospel; and the remnants of the seed of who were from Palestine and who colonized the shores of the Caspian Sea and thence made their way into the north of Europe, western Scandinavia and northern Germany, penetrating Scotland and England, and conquering those nations and reigning as monarchs of Great Britain, and mingling their seed with the Anglo-Saxon race, and spreading over the waters a fruitful vine, as predicted by Jacob, whose branches should run over the wall. Their blood has permeated European society, and it coursed in the veins of the early colonists of America. And when the books shall be opened and the lineage of all men is known, it will be found that they have been first

> and foremost in everything noble among men in the various nations in breaking off the shackles of kingcraft and priestcraft and oppression of every kind, and the foremost among men in upholding and maintaining the principles of liberty and freedom upon this continent and establishing a representative government, and thus preparing the way for the coming forth of the fullness of the everlasting Gospel. And it is the foremost of those spirits whom the Lord has prepared to receive the Gospel when it was presented to them, and who did not wait for the Elders to hunt them from the hills and corners of the earth, but they were hunting for the Elders, impelled by a spirit which then they could not understand; and for this reason were they among the first Elders of the Church; they and the fathers having been watched over from the days that God promised those blessings upon Isaac and Jacob and Joseph and Ephraim. And these are they that will be found in the front ranks of all that is noble and good in their day and time, and who will be found among those whose efforts are directed in establishing upon the earth those heaven-born principles which tend directly to blessing and salvation, to ameliorating the condition of their fellow-men, and elevating them in the scale of their being; and among those also who receive the fullness of the Everlasting Gospel, and the keys of Priesthood in the last days, through whom God determined to raise up again unto himself a peculiar people, a holy nation, a pure seed that shall stand upon Mount Zion as saviors, not only to the house of Israel but also to the house of Esau. (in *Journal of Discourses,* 23:183–84, 186–87)

Feelings of rivalry and bitterness have existed between the children of Isaac and those of the house of Ishmael. The descendants of Ishmael feel that they were, in a sense, robbed of sacred land by the descendants of Isaac. They believe that it was their father Ishmael, not Isaac, who was taken to Mt. Moriah to be sacrificed. On the other hand, the Jews, who are the descendants of Abraham as well, through Judah, a great-grandson of the patriarch, possess the land and are willing to stand at all costs to defend the land that they feel is rightfully theirs by inheritance from their forefathers. They bitterly fight today over those birthright inheritances. But what they both overlook is that it was Joseph to whom the true birthright fell, and it is to him that they both must ultimately come to receive their eternal inheritances.

Joseph's seed, Ephraim and Manasseh, were both part of the lost ten tribes, but the blood of both tribes has been scattered throughout the earth. Collectively, as a tribe, they are lost, but as prophesied, in the last days a remnant of Joseph's seed will be called and raised up to take their rightful place at the head of the seed of Abraham.

Prophecy also seems to indicate that much strife and loss of life will accompany the rivalry between Isaac's and Ishmael's descendants before the promised Messiah will raise up Ephraim and then return himself to reign supreme during the thousand years of peace. In reality they are all brothers and sisters of the same God and the same common forefather, though their versions of the details of the story differ. However, they both also need to understand that their other brothers and sisters of the house of Joseph have the pivotal role in this long and storied history. It is ultimately members of Ephraim who will need to stand in their place as holders of the holy priesthood at the head of the house of Abraham.

The most significant message that must permeate this whole discussion is that ultimately all of this grand family—Ishmael, Isaac, Judah, Joseph, and the rest of the tribes of Israel (upon their return from captivity)—as well as the rest of mankind, must learn to live together in love, cooperation, and mutual friendship in order for real, lasting peace to exist on the face of the earth and for the Messiah to be able to carry on the work of the salvation of the children of men. They must also come to understand the importance of the priesthood authority that the house of Joseph holds and why we must all come to him to obtain the ordinances of salvation through the holy priesthood if those ordinances are to be recognized by our Father in Heaven. When all of this happens, and only when it happens, will we all be able to dwell together in peace, each of us filling our role as children of the God our father Abraham worshipped and fulfilling the covenants that we all inherit through him.

Eventually every knee will bow and every tongue will confess that Jesus is the Christ, the Savior of the world. And eventually the strong wills of all of His prideful children will of necessity be turned from self to their God, who alone will rule supreme. It will be at that point that the scripture will be fulfilled concerning the reestablishing of the ancient covenants of Abraham with his latter-day seed:

> But now hath he obtained a more excellent ministry, by how much also he is the mediator of a better covenant, which was established upon better promises.
>
> For if that first covenant had been faultless, then should no place have been sought for the second.
>
> For finding fault with them, he saith, Behold, the days come, saith the Lord, when I will make a new covenant with the house of Israel and with the house of Judah:
>
> Not according to the covenant that I made with their fathers in the day when I took them by the hand to lead them out of the land of Egypt; because they continued not in my covenant, and I regarded them not, saith the Lord.
>
> For this is the covenant that I will make with the house of Israel after those days, saith the Lord; I will put my laws into their mind, and write them in their hearts: and I will be to them a God, and they shall be to me a people:
>
> And they shall not teach every man his neighbour, and every man his brother, saying, Know the Lord: for all shall know me, from the least to the greatest.
>
> For I will be merciful to their unrighteousness, and their sins and their iniquities will I

> remember no more. In that he saith, A new covenant, he hath made the first old. Now that which decayeth and waxeth old is ready to vanish away. (Hebrews 8:6–13)

This, then, will be the ultimate destiny of the seed of father Abraham. His scattered descendants will be reclaimed from the years of their separation from the covenants of their father's God, which occurred because of their disobedience. Then they will once again be a united people, both physically and, more important, in righteousness, to dwell in peace forever in the kingdom of their Heavenly Father.

ABRAHAM

ISAAC

JACOB (ISRAEL)

Tribes Separate in 925 B.C.

Northern Kingdom *(Israel)*	Southern Kingdom *(Judah)*
Reuben	Judah
Simeon	Benjamin
Levi (Aaronic Priesthood)	
Zebulun	Taken captive
Issachar	into Babylon
Dan	*(Jeremiah 52)*
Gad	(587 B.C.)
Asher	Commencement of
Naphtali	Persian Empire
Manasseh	(559 B.C.)
	Commissioned to
Joseph (birthright son)	rebuild Jerusalem
Ephraim	(Cyrus 537 B.C.)
	Persia conquered by Egypt
	(330 B.C.)
	Egypt becomes a Roman province
Taken captive,	(30 B.C.)
scattered, lost	Christ is born
(2 Kings 17)	

Remnant is spared *(1 Nephi 6:2)*
Scattered Israel to be gathered in the last days by Ephraim
(Ezekiel 37:14–28; Jeremiah 16:9–21)

Old Testament Prophets/Leaders Called

Northern Kingdom	Southern Kingdom	
1. Joshua	1. Ezra	10. Micah
2. Samuel	2. Nehemiah	11. Habakkuk
3. Ruth	3. Esther	12. Zephaniah
4. Elijah	4. Nathan	13. Haggai
5. Elisha	5. Isaiah	14. Zechariah
6. Amos	6. Jeremiah	15. Malachi
7. Obadiah	7. Ezekiel	
8. Jonah	8. Daniel	
9. Nahum	9. Joel	

Chapter 8

Adoption and Election

And now, because of the covenant which ye have made ye shall be called the children of Christ, his sons, and his daughters; for behold, this day he hath spiritually begotten you; for ye say that your hearts are changed through faith on his name; therefore, ye are born of him and have become his sons and his daughters.

And under this head ye are made free, and there is no other head whereby ye can be made free. There is no other name given whereby salvation cometh; therefore, I would that ye should take upon you the name of Christ, all you that have entered into the covenant with God that ye should be obedient unto the end of your lives.

—Mosiah 5:7–8

To redeem them that were under the law, that we might receive the adoption of sons. And because ye are sons, God hath sent forth the Spirit of his Son into your hearts, crying, Abba, Father. Wherefore thou art no more a servant, but a son; and if a son, then an heir of God through Christ.

—Galatians 4:5–7

Many couples, for varying reasons, are not able to conceive and have offspring of their own flesh and blood. Often these couples turn to adoption to fulfill their desire to be parents and have a family. When adoption is done through the proper process and through the authorized channels of the law, it becomes legally binding. Only then does the law recognize the adoption as an official act. When parents legally adopt a child, that child is considered a legal heir along with any physical offspring those parents may have. The fact that the child was physically begotten by different parents is irrelevant. An adopted child is considered part of the new family by the law.

When we understand that concept, we are in a position to be able to understand the doctrine of adoption as it is taught in the scriptures. In order to become part of the family of Jesus Christ (His sons and daughters), we must, of necessity, be adopted by Him. This process is accomplished through the ordinance of baptism, by a duly authorized holder of His priesthood, and by confirmation into His Church, which includes the bestowal of the Holy Ghost. The house of Israel was designated as His (God's) covenant family, so we must all become part of that family to obtain our salvation. Whether we were born into the church is irrelevant, so long as we become adopted sons and daughters of Christ by being adopted into the house of Israel.

This doctrine of spiritual adoption, is illustrated by President James E. Faust:

> Joseph Fielding Smith stated, "The great *majority* of those who become members of the Church are *literal descendants* of Abraham through Ephraim, son of Joseph." However, Manasseh, the other son of Joseph, as well as the other sons of Jacob, have many descendants in the Church. There may be some come into the Church in our day who are not of Jacob's blood lineage. No one need assume that he or she will be denied any blessing by reason of not being of the blood lineage of Israel. . . . Therefore, it makes no difference if the blessings of the house of Israel come by lineage or by adoption.
>
> Some might be disturbed because members

> of the same family have blessings declaring them to be of a different lineage. A few families are of a mixed lineage. We believe that the house of Israel today constitutes a large measure of the human family. Because the tribes have intermixed one with another, one child may be declared to be from the tribe of Ephraim, and another of the same family from Manasseh or one of the other tribes. The blessing of one tribe, therefore, may be dominant in one child, and the blessing of another tribe dominant yet in another child. So, children from the same parents could receive the blessings of different tribes. ("Priesthood Blessings," *Ensign,* November 1995, 64)

Only when we become one with the Savior and His Father do we qualify to return and live with them eternally. The Savior spoke of this process of becoming one in the greatest prayer ever uttered. Before He went to the Garden of Gethsemane to atone for the sins of the entire human race, He prayed fervently to His Father in Heaven for those whom His father had given to Him as adopted children:

> I have manifested thy name unto the men which thou gavest me out of the world: thine they were, and thou gavest them me; and they have kept thy word. Now they have known that all things whatsoever thou hast given me are of thee.
>
> For I have given unto them the words which thou gavest me; and they have received them, and have known surely that I came out from thee, and they have believed that thou didst send me.
>
> I pray for them: I pray not for the world, but for them which thou hast given me; for they are thine. And all mine are thine, and thine are mine; and I am glorified in them.
>
> And now I am no more in the world, but these

> are in the world, and I come to thee. Holy Father, keep through thine own name those whom thou hast given me, that they may be one, as we are.
>
> While I was with them in the world, I kept them in thy name: those that thou gavest me I have kept, and none of them is lost, but the son of perdition; that the scripture might be fulfilled.
>
> And now come I to thee; and these things I speak in the world, that they might have my joy fulfilled in themselves.
>
> I have given them thy word; and the world hath hated them, because they are not of the world, even as I am not of the world.
>
> I pray not that thou shouldest take them out of the world, but that thou shouldest keep them from the evil.
>
> They are not of the world, even as I am not of the world. Sanctify them through thy truth: thy word is truth. As thou hast sent me into the world, even so have I also sent them into the world.
>
> And for their sakes I sanctify myself, that they also might be sanctified through the truth. (John 17:6–19)

The Apostle Paul's teachings are replete with the doctrine of adoption as well:

> For as many as are led by the Spirit of God, they are the sons of God. For ye have not received the spirit of bondage again to fear; but ye have received the Spirit of adoption, whereby we cry, Abba, Father.
>
> The Spirit itself beareth witness with our spirit, that we are the children of God. . . . For we know that the whole creation groaneth and travaileth in pain together until now.

> And not only they, but ourselves also, which have the firstfruits of the Spirit, even we ourselves groan within ourselves, waiting for the adoption, to wit, the redemption of our body. (Romans 8:14–18, 22–23)

> For I could wish that myself were accursed from Christ for my brethren, my kinsmen according to the flesh: who are Israelites; to whom pertaineth the adoption, and the glory, and the covenants, and the giving of the law, and the service of God, and the promises;
>
> Whose are the fathers, and of whom as concerning the flesh Christ came, who is over all, God blessed for ever. Amen. (Romans 9:3–5)

> Now I say, That the heir, as long as he is a child, differeth nothing from a servant, though he be lord of all;
>
> But is under tutors and governors until the time appointed of the father. Even so we, when we were children, were in bondage under the elements of the world:
>
> But when the fulness of the time was come, God sent forth his Son, made of a woman, made under the law,
>
> To redeem them that were under the law, that we might receive the adoption of sons. And because ye are sons, God hath sent forth the Spirit of his Son into your hearts, crying, Abba, Father. (Galatians 4:1–6)

The Lord in His infinite wisdom set apart one special family as His family, and each of the human race must either be born into that family or be adopted into it through baptism if they expect to warrant eternal life with Him and His Father. Blood lineage is important, but the spiritual claim to the blessings of the house of Israel is essential.

The Christian world as a whole is in darkness as to the meaning of this vital doctrine. It is up to us who know of its truth to enlighten them concerning it. The question for us must be, do we ourselves understand how it all works? Whether one is born of the literal blood of Abraham or adopted into his family through baptism, it is the same. Each will receive equally the blessings of the Lord's covenant with them:

> Even as Abraham believed God, and it was accounted to him for righteousness.
>
> Know ye therefore that they which are of faith, the same are the children of Abraham.
>
> And the scripture, foreseeing that God would justify the heathen through faith, preached before the gospel unto Abraham, saying, In thee shall all nations be blessed.
>
> So then they which be of faith are blessed with faithful Abraham. (Galatians 3:6–9)

It is through this process that the promise made to Abraham can be fulfilled, that through his seed all of the nations and families of the earth would be blessed (Genesis 18:18; 26:3–4; 28:10–14; 48:18–22).

President Gordon B. Hinckley, in commenting on this doctrine, said: "I do not worry whether people are or are not literal descendants of Israel. Whether they got their blessings by inherited birthright or by adoption, the end result is the same—they become partakers of the everlasting covenant between Jehovah and Abraham, which extends to all of his posterity, whether by literal descent or by adoption" (*Stand a Little Taller,* 125).

When we speak of the doctrine of adoption, we must also of necessity understand the doctrine of election. Again, this is a doctrine stressed frequently, especially by the Apostle Paul in his writings. So, what is the doctrine of election? And how does it apply to the gospel of Jesus Christ?

We are told in the scriptures that we are to gather the elect from among all nations upon the earth:

> Verily, I say unto you that ye are chosen out

> of the world to declare my gospel with the sound of rejoicing, as with the voice of a trump.
>
> Lift up your hearts and be glad, for I am in your midst, and am your advocate with the Father; and it is his good will to give you the kingdom.
>
> And, as it is written—Whatsoever ye shall ask in faith, being united in prayer according to my command, ye shall receive.
>
> And ye are called to bring to pass the gathering of mine elect; for mine elect hear my voice and harden not their hearts. (D&C 29:4–7)

Elder Bruce R. McConkie spoke on the doctrine of election:

> The elect of God comprise a very select group, an inner circle of faithful members of The Church of Jesus Christ of Latter-day Saints. They are the portion of church members who are striving with all their hearts to keep the fulness of the gospel law in this life so that they can become inheritors of the fulness of gospel rewards in the life to come.
>
> As far as the male sex is concerned, they are the ones, the Lord says, who have the Melchizedek Priesthood conferred upon them and who thereafter magnify their callings and are sanctified by the Spirit. In this way, "They become the sons of Moses and of Aaron and the seed of Abraham, and the church and kingdom, and the elect of God." They keep "the oath and covenant which belongeth to the priesthood," and are rewarded with the fulness of the Father's kingdom. (D&C 84:33–41.)
>
> To gain this elect status they must be endowed in the temple of the Lord (D&C 95:8), enter into that "order of the priesthood" named "the new and

> everlasting covenant of marriage" (D&C 131:1–4), and overcome by faith until, as the sons of God, they merit membership in the Church of the Firstborn. (D&C 76:50–70, 94–96.) The elect of God are the chosen of God; and he has said: "There are many who have been ordained among you, whom I have called but few of them are chosen." (D&C 95:5; 121:34–40.)
>
> This is the day in which the Lord is gathering his, those who hear his voice and harden not their hearts (D&C 29:7), from the four quarters of the earth (D&C 33:6), so that if they continue to abide in his word, they have an eventual salvation in his presence. This is the day of which the Lord spoke: "I will bring forth a seed out of Jacob, and out of Judah an inheritor of my mountains: and mine elect shall inherit it, and my servants shall dwell there." (Isaiah 65:9.) The coming millennial day is one in which the "elect shall long enjoy the work of their hands" (Isaiah 65:22), for the earth and the fulness thereof shall then be theirs." (*Mormon Doctrine,* 218)

It appears that the elect are those who will hearken to the voice and teachings of the Savior when they are presented to them (John 10:24–27). The time and conditions of our births also appear not to have been a chance phenomenon:

> To carry forward his own purposes among men and nations, the Lord foreordained chosen spirit children in the pre-existence and assigned them to come to earth at particular times and places so that they might aid in furthering the divine will. These pre-existence appointments, made 'according to the foreknowledge of God the Father' (1 Peter 1:2), simply designated certain individuals to perform missions which the

> Lord in his wisdom knew they had the talents and capacities to do. . . .
>
> Israel is an eternal people. Members of that chosen race first gained their inheritance with the faithful in the pre-mortal life. Israel was a distinct people in the pre-existence. Many of the valiant and noble spirits in that first estate were chosen, elected, and foreordained to be born into the family of Jacob, so as to be natural heirs of all of the blessings of the gospel. It was to their pre-existent status that Moses alluded when, in speaking to mortal Israel, he said: "Remember the days of old, consider the years of many generations: ask thy father, and he will shew thee; thy elders, and they will tell thee. When the most High divided to the nations their inheritance, when he separated the sons of Adam, he set the bounds of the people according to the number of the children of Israel. For the Lord's portion is his people; Jacob is the lot of his inheritance." (Deuteronomy 32:7–9.) Those of mortal Israel who walk uprightly in this second estate shall have eternal inheritance with Israel in the world to come. (McConkie, *Doctrinal New Testament Commentary,* 2:268, 284)

Because we have been blessed of the Father, much will be required at our hands concerning how we have treated those special gifts of grace. President Harold B. Lee said:

> There are many among us who because of their faithfulness in the spirit world were "called" to do a great work here, but like reckless spendthrifts they are exercising their free agency in riotous living and are losing their birthright and the blessings that were theirs had they proved faithful to their calling." (*Youth and the Church,* 172)

Elder Bruce R. McConkie wrote:

> This election to a chosen lineage is based on pre-existent worthiness and is thus made "according to the foreknowledge of God." (1 Peter 1:2.) Those so grouped together during their mortal probation have more abundant opportunities to make and keep the covenants of salvation, a right which they earned by pre-existent devotion to the cause of righteousness. As part of this election, Abraham and others of the noble and great spirits were chosen before they were born for the particular missions assigned them in this life. (Abraham 3:22–24; Romans 9.) As with every basic doctrine of the gospel, the Lord's system of election based on pre-existent faithfulness has been changed and perverted by an apostate Christendom. So absurd have been the false conclusions reached in this field that millions of sincere though deceived persons have devoutly believed that in accordance with the divine will men were pre-destined to receive salvation or damnation which no act on their part could change. (*Teachings,* 189.)
>
> Actually, if the full blessings of salvation are to follow, the doctrine of election must operate twice. First, righteous spirits are elected or chosen to come to mortality as heirs of special blessings. Then, they must be called and elected again in this life, an occurrence which takes place when they join the true Church. (D&C 53:1.) Finally, in order to reap eternal salvation, they must press forward in obedient devotion to the truth until they make their "calling and election sure" (2 Peter 1), that is, are "sealed up unto eternal life" (D&C 131:5). (*Mormon Doctrine,* 216)

The Apostle Paul speaks of this doctrine continually throughout his writings (see Adoption/Election in Scripture Resources). It would seem apparent that the most important thing is that no matter what our condition at birth, we must become the elect of God through being humble, and thus teachable, if we expect to return and dwell with Him in His presence. Those who have been privileged to become the elect through their premortal faithfulness must remain the elect here in this second estate, if they are to attain eternal life. Meanwhile those who were not as fortunate must strive to become the elect while here in mortality if they wish to attain that same estate in the hereafter. Hence, we are foreordained, but not one of us is, as many in the Christian world deem, predestined. Ultimately, our Father has called us to be members of His eternal family, but it is up to us to make that foreordination a reality.

Chapter 9

Faith

And now as I said concerning faith—faith is not to have a perfect knowledge of things; therefore if ye have faith ye hope for things which are not seen, which are true.

—Alma 32:21

I recall hearing the story of a young boy who decided one afternoon to do some rock climbing with his friends. The friends got a bit too daring in their climbing, and in the midst of a bit of youthful nonchalance, he found himself on the edge of a rock ledge. Paralyzed by fear at the view presented to him there on the edge, he resisted the coaxing of his playmates to let them help him climb back down. Afternoon grew into evening, and he found himself facing his challenging predicament in darkness. Fear of the unknown gripped him, and tears filled his young eyes.

When it became obvious that he would not relent and heed his playmates' pleas, they left him and fled for help. They returned a short time later with the young boy's father, who approached the ledge where his young son was crouched in near-total darkness. Knowing of his child's fear, the father calmly called out to him. Upon hearing the familiar voice of his father, the boy called back that he couldn't see and was afraid.

His father's words gave him reassurance that he would be safe from harm. He knew that his father loved him and that he would do all within his power to deliver him from his plight. However, his father's next words brought with them an element of apprehension. "Son, I am here," he said. "I want you to let go of the ledge and jump. I will catch you." The prospect of such a move was almost more than this young boy could bear. Such an action on his part would require implicit trust and commitment and though the very thought of it made him tremble, this was his father and he believed in his ability to deliver him. Thus it was that he did as his father commanded: he let go and jumped. With his eyes closed tightly and a prayer in his heart he tumbled into his father's waiting arms. This story certainly illustrates true faith!

Elder Boyd K. Packer has commented on this important principle:

> Shortly after I was called as a General Authority, I went to Elder Harold B. Lee for counsel. He listened very carefully to my problem and suggested that I see President David O. McKay. President McKay counseled me as to the direction I should go. I was very willing to be obedient but saw no way possible for me to do as he counseled me to do.

> I returned to Elder Lee and told him that I saw no way to move in the direction I was counseled to go. He said, "The trouble with you is you want to see the end from the beginning." I replied that I would like to see at least a step or two ahead. Then came the lesson of a lifetime: "You must learn to walk to the edge of the light, and then a few steps into the darkness; then the light will appear and show the way before you." (*The Holy Temple,* 183–84)

The concept of faith is a broad one indeed. A couple of excellent definitions are given to us in the scriptures:

"Now faith is the substance of things hoped for, the evidence of things not seen" (Hebrews 11:1).

"And now as I said concerning faith—faith is not to have a perfect knowledge of things; therefore if ye have faith ye hope for things which are not seen, which are true" (Alma 32:21).

Faith is a critical requirement for each of us to obtain if we are to be accepted by our Savior as His children. We are told in the New Testament, "But without faith it is impossible to please him; for he that cometh to God must believe that he is, and that he is a rewarder of them that diligently seek him" (JST, Hebrews 11:6).

For the sake of an illustration, let's liken ourselves to the young boy stranded on the ledge and liken the father to our Heavenly Father and our elder brother Jesus Christ. At times in our lives we will find ourselves out on a ledge, so to speak, because of bad decisions or choices. The more we allow ourselves to backslide, the darker will be our surroundings.

When we finally come to our senses and realize that we are helpless to save ourselves, we hear our Father's voice call out of the darkness to let go of what it was that got us there and spiritually jump into His strong arms of peace and comfort. The prospects can be frightening, but if we expect to ever be delivered from our plight, we must trust enough in His words of counsel to let go of our worldly grip and jump.

Just as true safety did not come until the son acted upon his trust and belief in his father, so, likewise, we must act upon our hope, belief, and trust in our Father's promises and counsel if we are to truly manifest our faith. It's easy to talk a good game, but we don't possess true faith unless our actions manifest it.

Faith is a principle that is accepted by most Christian denominations. In fact, some denominations emphasize faith to the point that they believe that all they have to do to be partakers of salvation in its fullest form is merely to profess their faith in Christ with their lips. They use the words of Paul (such as found in his writings to the Saints at Ephesus) to support their premise:

> But God, who is rich in mercy, for his great love wherewith he loved us, even when we were dead in sins, hath quickened us together with Christ, (by grace ye are saved;)
>
> And hath raised us up together, and made us sit together in heavenly places in Christ Jesus: That in the ages to come he might shew the exceeding riches of his grace in his kindness toward us through Christ Jesus.
>
> For by grace are ye saved through faith; and that not of yourselves: it is the gift of God: Not of works, lest any man should boast. (Ephesians 2:4–9)

Those who focus their belief in salvation solely on the few scriptural passages of Paul in which he states that we are saved by grace would do well to consider his words in Romans 8 as well:

"For we are saved by hope: but hope that is seen is not hope: for what a man seeth, why doth he yet hope for? But if we hope for that we see not, then do we with patience wait for it" (Romans 8:24–25).

What, then, are we saved by? Is it by grace, or is it by hope? Or is it possible that we are saved by a combination of things, grace being the catalyst?

We are indeed saved by the grace of Jesus Christ. To deny that would be to embrace an incorrect premise. It would also appear that the key to that salvation is definitely connected to our attaining the faith necessary to facilitate it. Nonetheless, from some of the other writings of Paul and the writings of James, we see that faith alone is insufficient to warrant salvation. James explains that faith is action and must be accompanied by actual works to be fully realized and complete (James 2:13–26).

Two examples come to mind regarding the topic of faith. The first one tells of the centurion whose servant was ill and who went to the Savior requesting Him to heal the servant:

> The centurion answered and said, Lord, I am not worthy that thou shouldest come under my roof: but speak the word only, and my servant shall be healed.
>
> For I am a man under authority, having soldiers under me: and I say to this man, Go, and he goeth; and to another, Come, and he cometh; and to my servant, Do this, and he doeth it.
>
> When Jesus heard it, he marvelled, and said to them that followed, Verily I say unto you, I have not found so great faith, no, not in Israel. (Matthew 8:8–10)

This man's faith was so great that just the mere statement by the Savior that it would be done was good enough for him. If only the Master could speak likewise of each of us and our faith in such a complimentary manner!

The second example is from the Book of Mormon. The brother of Jared was facing an imposing dilemma. He had been asked by the Lord to cross the ocean in barges, which were going to be driven forth on the waters without any light in them. When he approached the Lord with the answer to the problem, he did so with such faith that the Lord revealed Himself to him:

> And it came to pass that when the brother of Jared had said these words, behold, the Lord stretched forth his hand and touched the stones one by one with his finger. And the veil was taken from off the eyes of the brother of Jared, and he saw the finger of the Lord; and it was as the finger of a man, like unto flesh and blood; and

> the brother of Jared fell down before the Lord, for he was struck with fear.
>
> And the Lord saw that the brother of Jared had fallen to the earth; and the Lord said unto him: Arise, why hast thou fallen?
>
> And he saith unto the Lord: I saw the finger of the Lord, and I feared lest he should smite me; for I knew not that the Lord had flesh and blood.
>
> And the Lord said unto him: Because of thy faith thou hast seen that I shall take upon me flesh and blood; and never has man come before me with such exceeding faith as thou hast; for were it not so ye could not have seen my finger. Sawest thou more than this?
>
> And he answered: Nay; Lord, show thyself unto me. And the Lord said unto him: Believest thou the words which I shall speak?
>
> And he answered: Yea, Lord, I know that thou speakest the truth, for thou art a God of truth, and canst not lie.
>
> And when he had said these words, behold, the Lord showed himself unto him, and said: Because thou knowest these things ye are redeemed from the fall; therefore ye are brought back into my presence; therefore I show myself unto you. (Ether 3:6–13)

The brother of Jared didn't ask the Lord what to do. Rather, he went to work, came up with a solution, and then went to the Lord for His help in seeing it through. I submit that within this story lies the true pattern of faith for each of us.

A number of years ago, I read a newspaper article about a man who had died after getting stuck in the mountains of Oregon. The headline to the article read, "Faith kept man from walking out after getting stranded in snowdrift." As I read the article, it occurred to me just how little many of us understand about the principle of faith. This man's truck had apparently become stuck in the snow while he was trying to drive the back roads over the Klamath Mountains. The man then "put his faith in God" and waited with the patience of Job for someone to rescue him.

This man sat in the cab of his pickup for nine weeks, checking off the calendar pages on his day planner and writing letters on a legal pad to his two sons, his fiancée, and his boss. The article's statement that I found so incredible was, "If he had only stepped out of the truck and followed the road back around a corner, he soon would have found clear pavement leading him down the mountain to safety."

What a needless tragedy! If only he had understood the principle of faith a little better, he would probably have survived. Let me illustrate what I mean by that statement by sharing some quotes from the man's daily journal, written during those nine weeks that he sat in his truck, wating to be saved:

(1) "I have no control over my life, it's all in His hands. . . . His will be done." (2) "Death here in a month or so, or He sends someone to save me. Yet knowing His will I'm at peace and His grace will prevail. If I'm saved to finish my life here, please know I'll always be thankful to you and remain your servant. If not . . . I'll see you in His glory."

There was no sign that he had ever left his truck in search of a way out of his predicament. Having been an avid outdoorsman all of my life, I understand that generally you're supposed to stay put when you get lost so that rescuers can have a better chance of finding you. But I am a bit puzzled at how a grown man could sit still for nine weeks and starve to death without at least venturing out a little at some point to try to help his situation! I have no doubt that this man was probably a religious man who thought he was indeed putting his trust in God to save him. But just believing didn't save him.

Depending on the weather, road workers said, he would have had to walk through snow for as little as a few hundred yards and for at most a few miles before hitting pavement. Snow never stays on that road anyplace but right there. All the man had to do was retrace his tire tracks, and he would have at least given himself a fighting chance to be saved.

This story would be quite amusing if it weren't so tragic. The misunderstanding that this man apparently had concerning the principle of faith cost him his life. In a similar light, the misunderstanding that many have concerning this vital principle of faith may well cost them eternal life. There is a fallacy in much of the Christian world that comes from misunderstanding the writings of the Apostle Paul. Many assume that passages such as "For by grace are ye saved through faith; and that not of yourselves: it is the gift of God: Not of works, lest any man should boast" (Ephesians 2:8–9) and "For God so loved the world, that he gave his only begotten Son, that whosoever believeth in him should not perish, but have everlasting life" (John 3:16) mean that all we must do to merit salvation is to simply profess a belief in Jesus Christ.

President N. Eldon Tanner said, "When we pray, it is important that we set about to do all in our power to make it possible for the Lord to answer our prayers. As my father said to me when I was just a boy, 'My son, if you want your prayers to be answered, you must get on your feet and do your part'" (in Conference Report, October 1967, 55). In other words, though salvation is surely a gift of grace, made possible through the atonement of Jesus Christ, it is nevertheless not a free ride for everybody. We must each qualify for that gift of grace by our accepting of the teachings and requirements set forth by the Savior. This fact is evidenced by other teachings given from Paul (see Redemption in Scripture Resources).

The Apostle Paul wrote his epistles, which he had organized while on one of his three missions, to various branches of the Church as well as to others who had received baptism from other authorized servants of the Lord. He had received either letters from them or word from other sources concerning problems that were arising concerning doctrines and practices that were entering into their worship. These letters, which make up much of the New Testament, are Paul's answers to those concerns and his counsel to the early Saints.

When we today, nearly two thousand years removed from their cultures and practices, attempt to interpret and assimilate Paul's teachings without a working knowledge of the particular problem or doctrine, we are running the risk of doing so incorrectly—that is, unless the same doctrines and practices are a part of our particular church. That is the claim of The Church of Jesus Christ of Latter-day Saints. It purports to be the same Church that was established by Jesus Christ during His mortal ministry. The years may have separated us from Paul's day, but the basic doctrines of the gospel of Jesus Christ are the same and will remain so eternally.

Knowing of the situation that would exist in the last days concerning the false interpretations of Paul's teachings, the Apostle Peter warned us of the inherent dangers of such interpretations:

> Wherefore, beloved, seeing that ye look for such things, be diligent that ye may be found of him in peace, without spot, and blameless.
>
> And account that the longsuffering of our Lord is salvation; even as our beloved brother Paul also according to the wisdom given unto him hath written unto you;
>
> As also in all his epistles, speaking in them of these things; in which are some things hard to be understood, which they that are unlearned and unstable wrest, as they do also the other scriptures, unto their own destruction.
>
> Ye therefore, beloved, seeing ye know these things before, beware lest ye also, being led away with the error of the wicked, fall from your own stedfastness. (2 Peter 3:14–17)

The book of James clarifies the importance of doing and becoming in addition to believing:

> What doth it profit, my brethren, though a man say he hath faith, and have not works? Can faith save him? Yea, a man may say, Thou hast faith, and I have works: shew me thy faith without thy works, and I will shew thee my faith by my works. Thou believest that there is one God; thou doest well: the devils also believe, and tremble. But wilt thou know, O vain man, that faith without works is dead? (James 2:14, 18–20)

Faith, therefore, becomes the beginning of our salvation, but our works will allow us to access the atonement of Jesus Christ and help us become who we need to be. Christ, then, become the finisher of our faith.

Chapter 10
Repentance

Come now, and let us reason together, saith the Lord: though your sins be as scarlet, they shall be as white as snow; though they be red like crimson, they shall be as wool.

—Isaiah 1:18

Behold, he who has repented of his sins, the same is forgiven, and I, the Lord, remember them no more. By this ye may know if a man repenteth of his sins—behold, he will confess them and forsake them.

—D&C 58:42–43

Of Satan's tools to lead men astray from the path of God, perhaps one of the most effective is that of shortsightedness: trading the things we will want the most later for things that look attractive right now. We would all be wise to bear in mind that none of us will escape the consequences of our actions.

Brazilians hold an annual celebration called Carnival. During the three-day period of this celebration, there is a prevailing belief that somehow God can't see what the people are doing. This results in a three-day sensual frenzy, apparently with the intent of tasting all of the forbidden fruit possible before God can once again see. It appears that those who participate in this ritual feel that there is no price for sin, unless one is caught in the act of committing it. Elder M. Russell Ballard has declared, "Sin will always, *always,* result in suffering. It may come sooner, or it may come later, but it will come" ("Purity Precedes Power," *Ensign,* May 1991, 7). Thus, when we have trespassed against the commands of the Lord we would be wise to rectify the situation as quickly and completely as possible.

One of the components of faith is action. None of us is free from sin (1 John 1:8), and therefore we all are in need of repentance. As we begin to obtain our faith, we need to take that faith to the next level by manifesting it through our actions. We aren't going to become a new person as to sin by merely believing, anymore than we will get well from an illness by merely getting a prescription from the doctor and carrying it around with us. We have to take the medication before it can begin to be any benefit to us. There are some things that we need to do as well if we are going to be cleansed from our sins, as expressed by Elder Francis M. Lyman: "Repentance is also a gift from the Lord, as precious as faith. We cannot be saved by faith alone. We must repent. Repentance is necessary to salvation. . . . There is no forgiveness of sin without repentance. Forgiveness does not come by faith alone, nor by promising that we will do better some time. It is necessary that we should cease sinning and begin to do well" (in Doxey, *Latter-day Prophets and the Doctrine and Covenants,* 2:300–301.)

I have observed a strange ritual over the years concerning the process of repentance. It seems as though we as a people have managed to program this process into a series of "steps" that must be completed before we can be forgiven of sin. I suppose that in theory this rationale has some merit, but in reality repentance is a lifelong process, not a checklist. To repent is to turn again toward God. If we have grown out of harmony with our Heavenly Father and our Savior, the process of repentance will allow us to regain that harmony. As in the case of the prodigal son, however, our deviation from the true path may result in blessings and opportunities being forever lost. President Spencer W. Kimball said:

> There is no justification for the inference that a repentant sinner is to be given precedence over a righteous soul who has resisted sin; were such the way of God, then Christ, the one sinless Man, would be surpassed in the Father's esteem by regenerate offenders. Unqualifiedly offensive as is sin, the sinner is yet precious in the Father's eyes, because of the possibility of his repentance and return to righteousness. The loss of a soul is a very real and a very great loss to God. He is pained and grieved thereby, for it is his will that not one should perish. (*Miracle of Forgiveness,* 309)

The parable of the prodigal son is a powerful story that teaches us important gospel principles:

> This superb parable . . . teaches the importance of remaining pure and undefiled and retaining virtue and righteousness; and it teaches the heavy penalties of transgression. It emphasizes the principle of repentance as a means of forgiveness and recovery of self. It teaches the ugliness of pride, jealousy, peevishness, lack of understanding, and anger; and it stresses the glorious and ultimate blessings, which are available to the worthy, even though they may exhibit some minor weaknesses.
>
> The prodigal son certainly had every opportunity to enjoy permanently a full and valuable

estate with resultant comforts, joys, harmony and peace. He had security. All was available to him until he left the path and dissipated his fortune, hating his birthright. He had demanded from his father, ". . . the portion of goods that falleth to me." He took it "all" into a far country, and there, pressed by the demands of a carnal world, wasted his substance with riotous living. He spent "all" of his estate and was reduced to penury and hunger.

He admitted rather than confessed his broken covenants. And what a difference between admission and confession! He acknowledged his unworthiness but said not a word about changing from unrighteousness to purity through a reformed life. "Coming to himself" seems to be more a realization of his physical plight, his hunger pangs and his unemployment, than a true repentance. Is there here any reference to new goals, a transformed life, escalating ideals and attitudes? He talked about bread of the oven rather than the "bread of life"—the water of the well rather than the "Living Water." He said nothing about filling a crown with jewels of righteous accomplishments, but made much of filling a stomach which was shriveled by near starvation.

The older son's being ever with his father is significant. If this parable is a reminder of life's journey, we remember that for the faithful who live the commandments there is a great promise of seeing the Lord and being with him always in exaltation. On the other hand, the younger son could hope for no more than salvation as a servant, since he "despised his birthright," and dissipated "all" of his inheritance, leaving nothing to develop and accumulate toward eternal heirship again. He had sold it for a mess of pottage as did

Esau, another prodigal.

He had sold something he could not recover. He had exchanged the priceless inheritance of great lasting value for a temporary satisfaction of physical desire, the future for the present, eternity for time, spiritual blessings for physical meat. Though he was sorry for his rash trade, it was now so late, "everlastingly too late." Apparently neither his efforts nor his tears could retrieve his lost blessings. Thus God will forgive the repentant sinner who sins against divine law, but that forgiveness can never restore the losses he sustained during the period of his sinning.

But many wrongs can be repaired if repentance is sincere. President Joseph F. Smith amplified this thought as follows:

"When we commit sin, it is necessary that we repent of it and make restitution as far as lies in our power. When we cannot make restitution for the wrong we have done, then we must apply for the grace and mercy of God to cleanse us from that iniquity.

"Men cannot forgive their own sins; they cannot cleanse themselves from the consequences of their sins. Men can stop sinning and can do right in the future, and so far their acts are acceptable before the Lord and worthy of consideration. But who shall repair the wrongs they have done to themselves and to others, which it seems impossible for them to repair themselves? By the atonement of Jesus Christ the sins of the repentant shall be washed away; though they be crimson they shall be made white as wool. This is the promise given to you. We who have not paid our tithing in the past, and are therefore under obligations to the Lord, which we are not in position to discharge, the Lord requires that

> no longer at our hands, but will forgive us for the past if we will observe this law honestly in the future. That is generous and kind, and I feel grateful for it." (Spencer W. Kimball, *Miracle of Forgiveness,* 309–11)

So what exactly is repentance? As we can see from these words, the Savior isn't as concerned as much with our past as He is with what we do with today, tomorrow, and the future. As mentioned before, the word *repent* means to turn to again. It should be remembered, however, that our past may cost us some of our inheritance.

Many years ago I knew a man who had been married in the temple to a great woman and who had a fine family. One evening as I was mowing my lawn I noticed him jogging out into the area of the neighboring fields. That didn't seem strange, as I had seen him do so on occasion, but what did strike me was that he was jogging with the neighbor's wife from across the street. It wasn't long until their temple marriages were in shambles. The two decided that they had married the wrong people, divorced their spouses, and then married each other. I was the ward Young Men president at the time, and the man's son told me of the seedy activities that his father had become involved in that led to the breaking of his temple covenants. Among those activities which was viewing hard-core pornographic movies in his home. The son told me that his father didn't think that he had done anything wrong.

After the breakup of these families, the father visited our ward on occasion. I sat in amazement on one such occasion in a Sunday School class and listened to him respond to a question posed by the instructor concerning some aspect of sin. He verbally blasted someone for a sin of much less magnitude than the one he had been involved in, yet he could not admit to himself that he had need of repentance. It became obvious to me that unless individuals are able to admit to themselves that they have committed sin, they cannot possibly begin to rectify their situation before God. *Recognition,* it appears, is the first element in the process of repentance.

Some years ago a student nearly floored me with her response to a lesson on repentance. After class she asked if she could talk to me for a minute in my office. I said that would be fine, and once we were in the office I asked her what was on her mind. She said, "My boyfriend and I have been sleeping together, and I am pregnant. And I'm not a bit sorry about it! What do you think about that?"

A bit taken aback by such a calloused declaration, I said, "Well, it doesn't really matter what I think about it because I'm not going to be your judge. It's what the Savior thinks that really matters. But you asked for my opinion, so let me give it to you straight and undiluted. With the attitude that you now have, it is impossible for you to repent. What you have done is a serious thing, and unless you repent, you can never be forgiven."

I then promised her that she would never be truly happy until she cleared herself of the sin that she had been committing. Unless individuals feel true remorse, or *godly sorrow,* for their sins, they can never truly repent of them.

A few years later I ran into her at a local grocery store. She hurried up to me with a young child at her heels and excitedly told me of how she and her husband were preparing to go to the temple and be sealed for time and all eternity. I told her how glad I was that she had turned her life around and how happy she looked. She then told me how good it felt to finally feel clean and free from the burdens she had formerly carried.

We all must come to the same conclusion if we are to have the burden of our sins removed from our shoulders. It isn't going to be enough to just be sorry that we got caught. We need to feel of the pain and suffering that our rebellious acts caused the Savior in the Garden of Gethsemane and then feel sorrow because we caused Him such pain. When we feel that kind of sorrow, we are ready to begin our repentance process.

The scriptures teach us that if a man truly is repentant he will confess his sins and forsake them (D&C 58:42–43). It is a difficult and humbling thing to face someone we may have wronged and acknowledge our guilt. *Humility* is a major requirement in the process of repentance, and perhaps that is why the Savior requires us to *confess our sins* before him. If our sins have been of a serious nature, such as moral transgressions, confession to the Lord's authorized servants is required.

Bishops are called as common judges in Israel and are authorized by the Lord to forgive the members of their wards on behalf of the Church. They must make judgments about a person's worthiness when it comes to serving in various capacities within the Church. We should remember, however, that ultimately we must confess all of our sins to Him who atoned for them if we want His forgiveness.

When our children were young they would occasionally do things that would hurt their brothers or sister. When these occasions arose, my wife and I required that they make things right with the offended sibling. Usually they would just say, "Sorry!" apparently thinking that somehow their profession of remorse would magically make everything all better. Children learn that magic word and think that by saying it, all will be forgiven, regardless of the situation or the offense. It is important to recognize that if we want to be forgiven, we must ask the injured one for forgiveness, not just merely say, "Sorry." Ultimately, forgiveness for every sin must be sought from the Savior because He suffered for all of our sins.

We should also *ask for forgiveness* from others whom our actions may have offended. When we have wronged others or taken something from them, we should do all in our power to restore the things that have been lost. Whether the loss was of a monetary nature or involved the loss of one's reputation or trust, we should try as much as possible to *make restitution* for that loss. Sometimes that just isn't possible, as in the case of the loss of chastity or life. That is why sins of that kind are in a class by themselves. In biblical times the Lord set the price of restitution high—and with interest!

> If a man shall steal an ox, or a sheep, and kill it, or sell it; he shall restore five oxen for an ox, and four sheep for a sheep.
>
> If a thief be found breaking up, and be smitten that he die, *there shall* no blood *be shed* for him.
>
> If the sun be risen upon him, *there shall be* blood *shed* for him; *for* he should make full restitution; if he have nothing, then he shall be sold for his theft.
>
> If the theft be certainly found in his hand alive, whether it be ox, or ass, or sheep; he shall restore double. (Exodus 22:1–4)

When people truly want to change their lives and turn them over to

Christ, there will an observable change in their behavior, actions, and language. Their lives will reflect that change of heart (Mosiah 5:2). They will feel an increased desire to *live all of the* commandments, and they will *forsake* their former sins. As a result of this spiritual rebirth, they should feel an increased desire to *share* with others the joy that *the gospel* has brought into their life.

This process of helping bring others to Christ will help them to receive and retain a remission of their sins (James 5:19–20). It should be noted, however, that the process of merely sharing the gospel with others does not by itself remit anyone's sins. We must all still go through the process of repentance and change if we expect to receive our covenant Father's forgiveness.

Chapter 11
Baptism

Therefore I give unto you a commandment, to teach these things freely unto your children, saying: That by reason of transgression cometh the fall, which fall bringeth death, and inasmuch as ye were born into the world by water, and blood, and the spirit, which I have made, and so became of dust a living soul, even so ye must be born again into the kingdom of heaven, of water, and of the Spirit, and be cleansed by blood, even the blood of mine Only Begotten; that ye might be sanctified from all sin, and enjoy the words of eternal life in this world, and eternal life in the world to come, even immortal glory.

—Moses 6:58–59

When a Pharisee named Nicodemus approached the Savior with the question of what he needed to do to inherit eternal life, Jesus gave what appeared to Nicodemus as a puzzling reply. He said:

> Verily, verily, I say unto thee, Except a man be born again, he cannot see the kingdom of God.
>
> Nicodemus saith unto him, How can a man be born when he is old? Can he enter the second time into his mother's womb, and be born?
>
> Jesus answered, Verily, verily, I say unto thee, Except a man be born of water and of the Spirit, he cannot enter into the kingdom of God.
>
> That which is born of the flesh is flesh; and that which is born of the Spirit is spirit. Marvel not that I said unto thee, Ye must be born again. (John 3:3–7)

The questions posed by this Pharisee were really not that strange. Once a person has been born into mortality, it would not make a lot of sense to go through that process again. The Savior taught the inhabitants of the ancient Americas that same doctrine:

> Behold, verily, verily, I say unto you, I will declare unto you my doctrine.
>
> And this is my doctrine, and it is the doctrine which the Father hath given unto me; and I bear record of the Father, and the Father beareth record of me, and the Holy Ghost beareth record of the Father and me; and I bear record that the Father commandeth all men, everywhere, to repent and believe in me.
>
> And whoso believeth in me, and is baptized, the same shall be saved; and they are they who shall inherit the kingdom of God. And whoso believeth not in me, and is not baptized, shall be damned.
>
> Verily, verily, I say unto you, that this is my

> doctrine, and I bear record of it from the Father; and whoso believeth in me believeth in the Father also; and unto him will the Father bear record of me, for he will visit him with fire and with the Holy Ghost. (3 Nephi 11:31–35)

What did the Savior mean in giving such an answer? How can the ordinance of baptism symbolically represent a rebirth? The ordinance of baptism is representative of being lowered into our earthly grave (being submerged in the water) and coming forth as a new person. However, if we are to fully understand the actual depth of the symbolism of the baptismal ordinance, we must examine the beginning of life and the process of physical birth.

From the moment of conception, life moves forth in a most miraculous manner. For the nine months that the unborn fetus resides safely within its mother's womb, it is encompassed in an environment of water. At the time of birth, those waters break, and the new human being comes forth as a living soul.

Along with the extrusion of water, another element is present in great abundance. That element is blood. And it is at this point that the mother puts her very life in the balance for the opportunity of giving her offspring life. The mother gives her own blood to provide life for her newborn child.

What then is there in the ordinance of baptism that would symbolize an individual's rebirth? Let us explore this doctrine in a manner that perhaps will solve some of the confusion experienced in Christianity today.

We will use the mortal birth experience as our model in this explanation, because it is the likeness that the Savior chose to use. When we commit any sin, we become unclean, and, therefore, we are unworthy to be in the presence of our Heavenly Father or His son Jesus Christ. There is really no way that makes any sense, as humans would reason, for us to undo the transgressions of our past. The prophet Nephi explained:

"But behold, I say unto you, the kingdom of God is not filthy, and there cannot any unclean thing enter into the kingdom of God; wherefore there must needs be a place of filthiness prepared for that which is filthy" (1 Nephi 15:34).

So where does this fact leave us? We have all sinned, and therefore we don't measure up to God's holiness. "For all have sinned, and come short of the glory of God" (Romans 3:23). Are we therefore damned to an everlasting hell? Since we can't, as Nicodemus so aptly stated, return and be born a second time from our earthly mother's womb, what does it mean to be "born again"? We must look at the symbolism intended in the ordinance of baptism if we are going to understand the answer to that question.

The doctrine of baptism has generated diverse views. Some feel that it must be done by immersion to be valid. Another school of Christian belief teaches that it is to be done by sprinkling. Still another view is that we don't need to have it done as a physical ordinance at all, but rather, that it is a condition of the heart or the spirit. The symbolism is the key to understanding the true doctrine concerning why the Savior taught what He taught.

Just as we emerge from our mother's womb, from an environment of total dependence on the one whose sacrifice will give us life, so also will we gain spiritual life as we experience rebirth through the one who has the power to give us that life. When we are baptized we must be immersed totally in water, and come forth out of the watery grave, just as we came forth from total immersion in the womb. It should be quite obvious for us to see the symbolism in this. How would sprinkling symbolize that first birth process? Frankly, it doesn't. That would also rule out the philosophy that all we must experience is merely a baptism of the heart or mind.

Just as we are born of water, we must also be born of the spirit and cleansed in the blood of the Lamb. Being born of the Holy Ghost is likened in the scriptures as being born of fire: "I indeed baptize you with water unto repentance: but he that cometh after me is mightier than I, whose shoes I am not worthy to bear: he shall baptize you with the Holy Ghost, and with fire" (Matthew 3:11).

Fire is perhaps the best cleansing agent. When something has been contaminated, we burn it if we want to ensure that the contaminant is eliminated. Perhaps that is why the Savior uses that imagery to describe the process of sanctification, which is accomplished through the cleansing power of the Holy Ghost. When we have truly been born again of the Holy Ghost, we will have sin purged from our very souls. We will be as the people of Nephi at the time of the reign of King Benjamin:

And now, it came to pass that when king Benjamin had made an end of speaking the words which had been delivered unto him by the angel of the Lord, that he cast his eyes round about on the multitude, and behold they had fallen to the earth, for the fear of the Lord had come upon them.

And they had viewed themselves in their own carnal state, even less than the dust of the earth. And they all cried aloud with one voice, saying: O have mercy, and apply the atoning blood of Christ that we may receive forgiveness of our sins, and our hearts may be purified; for we believe in Jesus Christ, the Son of God, who created heaven and earth, and all things; who shall come down among the children of men.

And it came to pass that after they had spoken these words the Spirit of the Lord came upon them, and they were filled with joy, having received a remission of their sins, and having peace of conscience, because of the exceeding faith which they had in Jesus Christ who should come, according to the words which king Benjamin had spoken unto them.

And king Benjamin again opened his mouth and began to speak unto them, saying: My friends and my brethren, my kindred and my people, I would again call your attention, that ye may hear and understand the remainder of my words which I shall speak unto you.

For behold, if the knowledge of the goodness of God at this time has awakened you to a sense of your nothingness, and your worthless and fallen state—

I say unto you, if ye have come to a knowledge of the goodness of God, and his matchless power, and his wisdom, and his patience, and his long-

> suffering towards the children of men; and also, the atonement which has been prepared from the foundation of the world, that thereby salvation might come to him that should put his trust in the Lord, and should be diligent in keeping his commandments, and continue in the faith even unto the end of his life, I mean the life of the mortal body—
>
> I say, that this is the man who receiveth salvation, through the atonement which was prepared from the foundation of the world for all mankind, which ever were since the fall of Adam, or who are, or who ever shall be, even unto the end of the world.
>
> And this is the means whereby salvation cometh. And there is none other salvation save this which hath been spoken of; neither are there any conditions whereby man can be saved except the conditions which I have told you. . . .
>
> And now, it came to pass that when king Benjamin had thus spoken to his people, he sent among them, desiring to know of his people if they believed the words which he had spoken unto them.
>
> And they all cried with one voice, saying: Yea, we believe all the words which thou hast spoken unto us; and also, we know of their surety and truth, because of the Spirit of the Lord Omnipotent, which has wrought a mighty change in us, or in our hearts, that we have no more disposition to do evil, but to do good continually. (Mosiah 4:1–9; 5:1–2)

A truly life-changing metamorphosis will involve much more than the simple profession of our loyalty and acceptance of Jesus Christ and His way. It appears that the more "born again" we become, the more we will abhor sin. Even the thought of sin will make us cringe. Therefore, I would submit that this analogy is a fairly good barometer of the depth of our conversion. When we encounter anything that is contrary to the things that will allow us to enjoy the companionship of the Holy Ghost, we ought to find them repugnant. The degree to which this occurs within us seems to be a good gauge of the level of our conviction and rebirth.

Now, let us discuss the second part of the equation, the symbolism of blood. How can the process allow us to be cleansed by the blood that was so freely spilt in the garden and later on the cross by our Savior? Being cleansed by blood would appear to be an oxymoron, for there are few things that stain more permanently than blood. Let's examine what is implied by this unusual symbolism:

> And when ye spread forth your hands, I will hide mine eyes from you: yea, when ye make many prayers, I will not hear: your hands are full of blood.
>
> Wash you, make you clean; put away the evil of your doings from before mine eyes; cease to do evil; learn to do well; seek judgment, relieve the oppressed, judge the fatherless, plead for the widow.
>
> Come now, and let us reason together, saith the Lord: though your sins be as scarlet, they shall be as white as snow; though they be red like crimson, they shall be as wool. (Isaiah 1:15–18)

How could blood purify rather than stain? Well, physically it wouldn't. But again, if we look at the symbolism here, we will begin to understand. Blood is a unique component of the mortal body. It is the corruptible part of our body that carries impurities throughout it. On the other hand, it is also the part that carries healing properties throughout our body. Blood serves us in this life in three main ways: First, it cleanses our body. Second, it gives our body nourishment (oxygen and food). And third, it fights disease and infection in our body. If we lose our blood, we cease to live. We require blood transfusions when our blood supply is depleted beyond a certain point. If our body is ill, our blood has the ability to cleanse and heal us.

In a sense, we could liken the process of baptism to a cleansing blood transfusion donated by our Savior. In this scenario, He alone has the blood type compatible with each of ours, capable of restoring life in the face of otherwise certain eternal death and damnation.

The prophet Enoch, speaking of the things that his forefather Adam was taught by the Lord, illustrated this doctrine in Moses 6:

> Therefore I give unto you a commandment, to teach these things freely unto your children, saying: That by reason of transgression cometh the fall, which fall bringeth death, and inasmuch as ye were born into the world by water, and blood, and the spirit, which I have made, and so became of dust a living soul, even so ye must be born again into the kingdom of heaven, of water, and of the Spirit, and be cleansed by blood, even the blood of mine Only Begotten; that ye might be sanctified from all sin, and enjoy the words of eternal life in this world, and eternal life in the world to come, even immortal glory;
>
> For by the water ye keep the commandment; by the Spirit ye are justified, and by the blood ye are sanctified;
>
> Therefore it is given to abide in you; the record of heaven; the Comforter; the peaceable things of immortal glory; the truth of all things; that which quickeneth all things, which maketh alive all things; that which knoweth all things, and hath all power according to wisdom, mercy, truth, justice, and judgment.
>
> And now, behold, I say unto you: This is the plan of salvation unto all men, through the blood of mine Only Begotten, who shall come in the meridian of time. (Moses 6:58–62)

The Savior also taught the ancient Nephites concerning the manner of baptism:

> And the Lord said unto him: I give unto you power that ye shall baptize this people when I am again ascended into heaven.
>
> And again the Lord called others, and said unto them likewise; and he gave unto them power to baptize. And he said unto them: On this wise shall ye baptize; and there shall be no disputations among you.
>
> Verily I say unto you, that whoso repenteth of his sins through your words, and desireth to be baptized in my name, on this wise shall ye baptize them—Behold, ye shall go down and stand in the water, and in my name shall ye baptize them.
>
> And now behold, these are the words which ye shall say, calling them by name, saying:
>
> Having authority given me of Jesus Christ, I baptize you in the name of the Father, and of the Son, and of the Holy Ghost. Amen.
>
> And then shall ye immerse them in the water, and come forth again out of the water. (3 Nephi 11:21–26)

Jesus Christ was the perfect example to all of us in that he was baptized but was without sin. He taught us that baptism is an ordinance that all must receive. Even Adam was baptized to fulfill all the requirements for salvation. After being driven from the Garden of Eden, he and Eve were taught the gospel and commanded in turn to teach it to their posterity. Just as each of us must be baptized, so Adam was baptized:

> And it came to pass, when the Lord had spoken with Adam, our father, that Adam cried unto the Lord, and he was caught away by the Spirit of the Lord, and was carried down into the water, and was laid under the water, and was brought forth out of the water.
>
> And thus he was baptized, and the Spirit of

God descended upon him, and thus he was born of the Spirit, and became quickened in the inner man.

And he heard a voice out of heaven, saying: Thou art baptized with fire, and with the Holy Ghost. This is the record of the Father, and the Son, from henceforth and forever;

And thou art after the order of him who was without beginning of days or end of years, from all eternity to all eternity.

Behold, thou art one in me, a son of God; and thus may all become my sons. Amen. (Moses 6:64–68)

Chapter 12

The Gift of the Holy Ghost

Wherefore, now after I have spoken these words, if ye cannot understand them it will be because ye ask not, neither do ye knock; wherefore, ye are not brought into the light, but must perish in the dark. For behold, again I say unto you that if ye will enter in by the way, and receive the Holy Ghost, it will show unto you all things what ye should do.

—2 Nephi 32:4–5

A number of years ago while I was teaching a seminary class, I experienced something quite by accident that illustrates the reception of the Holy Ghost. I had been listening to the radio before class had started and thought that I had turned it off when class began because I couldn't hear anything coming from the speakers. At a certain juncture during the lesson I went over to play one of the media clips from the outline, and as I reached to push play on the VCR, the radio came on. It startled me and amused my students! I quickly recoiled, not knowing quite what had happened. As I again reached out to push play, the radio again began to play. By this time I had the students' attention, and the thought came to me to roll with the whole thing. So I did just that.

If I remember right, we had been discussing different aspects of prayer and how our Father in Heaven often answers our prayers through the whisperings of the Spirit. Then a marvelous analogy burst into my mind. My body was actually working as an antenna for the radio, and if I was away from the radio, we wouldn't be able to tell that it was even on. However, as I got close to it, my body allowed the radio signal to be recognizable. I explained to the students that in the same manner we often assume that we are not receiving answers to our prayers, when actually we are not tuned to the right frequency or have a bad connection in our receiver. In reality, the signal was there all along—we just weren't tuned into it.

It was a great analogy—useful in teaching the principle, though I hadn't ever really thought of it quite that way before. I had actually been given what to say precisely when I needed it. I have often pondered long and hard over decisions, as most of us have. I've also thought of how great it would be to have all of life's solutions come as conveniently as that analogy came.

In a world fraught with so many critical decisions, what would it be worth to have an adviser who could successfully guide us to make the best decisions in every case? With the volatility of the stock market, for example, such an adviser would be invaluable. But alas, if wishes were fishes, we'd probably all be experienced fishermen. A psychic hot line can't provide such valuable information for us, nor can any other medium that may claim to do so. There just is no foolproof quick fix to life's perplexing questions. Unfortunately, nobody knows everything. Well, almost nobody.

There is one adviser who can help us avoid making serious mistakes in this life. This someone will, if we give heed, lead us to happiness in this life and eternal life in the hereafter. Who is this perfect adviser?

> Do ye not remember that I said unto you that after ye had received the Holy Ghost ye could speak with the tongue of angels? And now, how could ye speak with the tongue of angels save it were by the Holy Ghost?
>
> Angels speak by the power of the Holy Ghost; wherefore, they speak the words of Christ. Wherefore, I said unto you, feast upon the words of Christ; for behold, the words of Christ will tell you all things what ye should do.
>
> For behold, again I say unto you that if ye will enter in by the way, and receive the Holy Ghost, it will show unto you all things what ye should do. (2 Nephi 32:2–3, 5)

Elder Marion G. Romney on one occasion gave some pertinent advice concerning the workings of the Holy Spirit: "I tell you that you can make every decision of your life correctly if you can learn to follow the guidance of the Holy Spirit. This you can do if you will discipline yourself to yield your own feelings to the promptings of the Spirit" (in Conference Report, October 1961, 61).

President John Taylor said the following regarding this principle: "And hence the necessity all the day long, and every day, and every week, month, and year, and under all circumstances, of men leaning upon the Lord and being guided by that Spirit that flows from Him, that we may not fall into error—that we may neither do anything wrong, say anything wrong, nor think anything wrong, and at all times retain that spirit" (*Journal of Discourses*, 6:106). This is a great truth, but the question remains: how do we achieve that goal?

Before His ascension, the Savior promised His disciples that though He would be leaving them, they would not be left alone. He informed them that He would give them a Comforter, a gift to help them in their times of need. Up to this point in the Savior's ministry, the Holy Ghost had been shed upon people at various times but only for the express purpose of verifying truth. The Savior promised that, at some point, it would be given in a greater capacity.

The first major documented fulfillment of this gift occurred at the Day of Pentecost, when amazing manifestations of this sacred power were poured out upon the congregation. People prophesied of great events, and the gift of tongues was made manifest (Acts 2).

The Holy Ghost is the third member of the Godhead and is a personage of spirit. Were that not so, He could not dwell within us (D&C 130:22). He has a number of duties, among them to testify of truth, to give us peace, to teach us and bring things to our remembrance, and to give us protection, both physical and spiritual.

Many people have been blessed by the power of the Holy Ghost. The power of the Holy Ghost is meant to be an aid to any sincere seeker of truth. It will enlighten our mind and witness to us of things that are true. However, it is not the power of the Holy Ghost that is of particular concern here but rather the gift of the Holy Ghost. There is a marked difference in the two manifestations, which is important to understand. To illustrate the gift of the Holy Ghost, let's look at two incidents in the New Testament.

> But when they believed Philip preaching the things concerning the kingdom of God, and the name of Jesus Christ, they were baptized, both men and women.
>
> Then Simon himself believed also: and when he was baptized, he continued with Philip, and wondered, beholding the miracles and signs which were done.
>
> Now when the apostles which were at Jerusalem heard that Samaria had received the word of God, they sent unto them Peter and John:
>
> Who, when they were come down, prayed for them, that they might receive the Holy Ghost:
>
> (For as yet he was fallen upon none of them: only they were baptized in the name of the Lord Jesus.)

> Then laid they their hands on them, and they received the Holy Ghost. And when Simon saw that through laying on of the apostles' hands the Holy Ghost was given, he offered them money,
>
> Saying, Give me also this power, that on whomsoever I lay hands, he may receive the Holy Ghost.
>
> But Peter said unto him, Thy money perish with thee, because thou hast thought that the gift of God may be purchased with money.
>
> Thou hast neither part nor lot in this matter: for thy heart is not right in the sight of God (Acts 8:12–21).

Note that it wasn't until after Peter had laid hands on their heads that the converts received the Holy Ghost. This bestowal is a gift that can only be conferred by a holder of the holy priesthood, and it is not bestowed until after a person's baptism. A second example involves the Apostle Paul while on one of his three missionary journeys:

> And it came to pass, that, while Apollos was at Corinth, Paul having passed through the upper coasts came to Ephesus: and finding certain disciples,
>
> He said unto them, Have ye received the Holy Ghost since ye believed? And they said unto him, We have not so much as heard whether there be any Holy Ghost.
>
> And he said unto them, Unto what then were ye baptized? And they said, Unto John's baptism.
>
> Then said Paul, John verily baptized with the baptism of repentance, saying unto the people, that they should believe on him which should come after him, that is, on Christ Jesus.
>
> When they heard this, they were baptized in the name of the Lord Jesus.

> And when Paul had laid his hands upon them, the Holy Ghost came on them; and they spake with tongues, and prophesied. (Acts 19:1–6)

After baptism each convert is confirmed a member of the Church by the laying on of hands and is given the gift of the Holy Ghost by an authorized priesthood holder. The gift of the Holy Ghost is meant to be with us as our constant companion, as long as we live worthily of its companionship. When we learn to walk by the Spirit, we need never make a mistake. We are also told in the scriptures that the Lord said, "I will forgive thee and thy brethren of their sins; but thou shalt not sin any more, for ye shall remember that my Spirit will not always strive with man; wherefore, if ye will sin until ye are fully ripe ye shall be cut off from the presence of the Lord" (Ether 2:15).

If we are going to retain the companionship of the Holy Ghost at all times, we must observe the laws of God concerning purity, virtue, honesty, and holiness, and by living in accordance with the commandments and teachings of the restored gospel of Jesus Christ. If we will learn to live by the Holy Ghost's guiding influence, we can find our way through the darkness of the day in which we live.

Elder Richard G. Scott said:

> You may have been prompted to abandon a debilitating part of your current life or to set in order an unwholesome habit that has begun to take root only to later produce bitter fruit. Likely there are some who have resolved to repent of serious mistakes and return to the refreshing waters of righteousness. These impressions to improve come from the Savior through the Holy Ghost. . . .
>
> With the gift of the Holy Ghost comes the ability to develop a powerfully sensitive capacity to make the right choices. Cultivate that gift. As the Lord has said, that is accomplished by consistent, righteous living. As you enhance your capacity to sense the direction of that infallible

> influence, you will avoid disappointment, discouragement, and even tragedy. . . .
>
> It is wondrously simple and so incomparably beautiful. As you continue to live righteously, you will always know what to do. Sometimes the discovery of that may require significant effort and trust on your part. Yet you will recognize what to do as you meet the conditions for such divine guidance in your life: obedience to the commandments of the Lord, trust in His plan, and the avoidance of anything that is contrary to it. The more closely you conform your life to the doctrine of the Lord, the more capacity you will have to do what the Spirit inspires you to do. . . .
>
> Joseph Smith was helped to accomplish tasks that were completely beyond his personal capacity. At times, this came through direct guidance and intervention. Yet often it was the quiet prompting of the Spirit and the accompanying support that came because of his obedience, his faith in the Master, and his unwavering determination to do His will. Why was he so successful? A portion of that answer comes in his personal declaration, "I made this my rule: *When the Lord commands, do it.*"
>
> I testify that within your own personal sphere of activity and framework of responsibilities, the Lord will provide that same help. When needed and earned, you can enjoy divine inspiration to know what to do and, when necessary, power or capacity to accomplish it. ("He Lives," *Ensign,* November 1999, 87–88).

What a superb promise! Elder Scott, in his humble manner, gave us the key to being able to avoid life's major pitfalls. It comes through possessing the gift of the Holy Ghost. It is a gift of inestimable value to each of us in our lives *if* we have had it bestowed upon us and *if* we live worthy of its presence. The Holy Ghost is the medium by which the Savior bestows his gifts of grace upon us.

An important factor in being able to draw upon the powers of Heaven in our daily lives is our willingness to come before the Savior each Sunday and make an accounting of the previous week by partaking of the emblems of the sacrament. At baptism we make covenants with Him, and it is through the taking of the sacrament that we renew those sacred covenants: to take His name upon us, keep His commandments, always remember Him, help bear one another's burdens that they may become light, and stand as a witness of God at all times, in all things, and in all places, even until death.

Each week we come to the sacrament table, and we must of necessity then take stock of our life for the past week. We should humbly review the events of the week, recommitting ourselves to live up to our part of that baptismal covenant. In the sacrament prayers is a key phrase that contains the help of which I speak: "that they may always have his Spirit to be with them" (D&C 20:77). That is the Lord's part of the covenant each week—in our behalf.

If we are willing to try to do our part, even though we will generally come up short, He will send us His Spirit to help us think and live appropriately during the upcoming week. As we strive to live in this manner week to week, the Lord promises, "Then shall thy confidence wax strong in the presence of God; and the doctrine of the priesthood shall distil upon thy soul as the dews from heaven. The Holy Ghost shall be thy constant companion, and thy scepter an unchanging scepter of righteousness and truth; and thy dominion shall be an everlasting dominion, and without compulsory means it shall flow unto thee forever and ever" (D&C 121:45–46).

I submit that when the Holy Ghost becomes our constant companion, we will begin to truly become born again because when we have the Spirit with us, we won't want to sin. In fact, even the very thought of sin will make us cringe. Our challenge is to live in this manner week to week, to perfect our lives, line upon line, precept upon precept, using the gift of His spirit until we can finally present our best selves unto him and so He can then be the finisher of our faith. Retaining the Holy Ghost as our constant companion is the key to our quest for perfection, for without it we will surely not survive the onslaught of evil that surrounds us every day.

In conclusion, I share the words of President James E. Faust:

> The comforting spirit of the Holy Ghost can abide with us twenty-four hours a day: when we work, when we play, when we rest. Its strengthening influence can be with us year in and year out. That sustaining influence can be with us in joy and in sorrow, when we rejoice as well as when we grieve. The Holy Ghost is the greatest guarantor of inward peace in our unstable world. (Faust, *Reach Up for the Light,* 116–23)

Chapter 13
The Ordinances of Salvation

In the celestial glory there are three heavens or degrees; and in order to obtain the highest, a man must enter into this order of the priesthood [meaning the new and everlasting covenant of marriage]; and if he does not, he cannot obtain it. He may enter into the other, but that is the end of his kingdom; he cannot have an increase. The more sure word of prophecy means a man's knowing that he is sealed up unto eternal life, by revelation and the spirit of prophecy, through the power of the Holy Priesthood.

—D&C 131:1–5

Of critical importance to each person's salvation is the obtaining of priesthood ordinances. The ancient prophet Nephi put it this way:

"And now, my beloved brethren, after ye have gotten into this strait and narrow path, I would ask if all is done? Behold, I say unto you, Nay; for ye have not come thus far save it were by the word of Christ with unshaken faith in him, relying wholly upon the merits of him who is mighty to save. Wherefore, ye must press forward with a steadfastness in Christ" (2 Nephi 31:19–20).

Once we have received the ordinance of baptism, we have just begun the quest for eternal life. Baptism is the door that each of us must pass through to get onto the path of exaltation, but it is just the first step in that progression. After our baptism, we must still enter into the other saving ordinances of the gospel—ordinances performed by holders of the priesthood.

Peter referred to the holders of the Savior's holy priesthood thus: "But ye are a chosen generation, a royal priesthood, an holy nation, a peculiar people; that ye should shew forth the praises of him who hath called you out of darkness into his marvellous light: which in time past were not a people, but are now the people of God: which had not obtained mercy, but now have obtained mercy" (1 Peter 2:9–10).

In ancient times the premortal Savior sought to endow the children of Israel with power from on high, but because of their lack of readiness, He instead gave them a series of rituals (the law of Moses) and later took Moses from their midst. When we enter into the ordinances and covenants of the higher priesthood, we are held to a stricter standard of conduct than those who have not received the priesthood. Though the Savior wants each of us to obtain this endowment of power, it is vital that we be prepared to live up to priesthood covenants before we enter into them so as not to condemn ourselves. This principle is taught in the Doctrine and Covenants.

> Priesthood continueth in the church of God in all generations, and is without beginning of days or end of years.
>
> And the Lord confirmed a priesthood also upon Aaron and his seed, throughout all their

generations, which priesthood also continueth and abideth forever with the priesthood which is after the holiest order of God.

And this greater priesthood administereth the gospel and holdeth the key of the mysteries of the kingdom, even the key of the knowledge of God.

Therefore, in the ordinances thereof, the power of godliness is manifest. And without the ordinances thereof, and the authority of the priesthood, the power of godliness is not manifest unto men in the flesh; for without this no man can see the face of God, even the Father, and live.

Now this Moses plainly taught to the children of Israel in the wilderness, and sought diligently to sanctify his people that they might behold the face of God;

But they hardened their hearts and could not endure his presence; therefore, the Lord in his wrath, for his anger was kindled against them, swore that they should not enter into his rest while in the wilderness, which rest is the fulness of his glory.

Therefore, he took Moses out of their midst, and the Holy Priesthood also; and the lesser priesthood continued, which priesthood holdeth the key of the ministering of angels and the preparatory gospel;

Which gospel is the gospel of repentance and of baptism, and the remission of sins, and the law of carnal commandments, which the Lord in his wrath caused to continue with the house of Aaron among the children of Israel until John, whom God raised up, being filled with the Holy Ghost from his mother's womb. . . .

For whoso is faithful unto the obtaining

> these two priesthoods of which I have spoken, and the magnifying their calling, are sanctified by the Spirit unto the renewing of their bodies.
>
> They become the sons of Moses and of Aaron and the seed of Abraham, and the church and kingdom, and the elect of God.
>
> And also all they who receive this priesthood receive me, saith the Lord. (D&C 84:17–27, 33–35)

From these verses we learn that there was a purpose to all that transpired in the story of the exodus of ancient Israel. What then was that purpose?

The priesthood of God is the power and authority of God the Father, given to man to act in His name and have it recognized and binding in His sight. President John Taylor said this concerning the priesthood:

> I shall briefly answer that it is the government of God, whether on the earth or in the Heavens, for it is by that power, agency, or principle that all things are governed on the earth and in the heavens, and by that power that all things are upheld and sustained. It governs all things—it directs all things—it sustains all things—and has to do with all things that God and truth are associated with. It is the power of God delegated to intelligences in the heavens and to men on the earth; and when we arrive in the celestial kingdom of God, we shall find the most perfect order and harmony existing, because there is the perfect pattern, the most perfect order of government carried out, and when or wherever those principles have been developed in the earth, in proportion as they have spread and been acted upon, just in that proportion have they produced blessings and salvation to the human family. (*Gospel Kingdom,* 129)

It is through the administration of the ordinances of the holy priesthood of God that each of us must obtain the covenants necessary for our salvation. President Taylor added, "Priesthood is . . . the principle and power by which [God] regulates, controls, dictates and manages His affairs , His worlds, His kingdoms, His principalities, His powers, His intelligences, and all things that are underneath Him and above Him, and with which He has to do" (John Taylor, *Deseret News* [Weekly], 28 December 1859, 338).

Elder Boyd K. Packer stated:

> "How often have you heard . . . the parallel path to heaven philosophy? [the belief that all churches lead to heaven]. They claim one church is not really better than another, just different. Eventually the paths will converge. One is, therefore, quite as safe in any church as another.
>
> While this seems to be very generous, it just cannot be true. . . . Suppose schools were operated on that philosophy, with each discipline a separate path leading to the same diploma. No matter whether you study or not, pass the tests or not, all would be given the same diploma—the one of their choice.
>
> Without qualifying, one could choose the diploma of an attorney, an engineer, a medical doctor. Surely you would not submit yourself to surgery under the hands of a graduate of that kind of school!
>
> But it does not work that way. It cannot work that way—not in education, not in spiritual matters. There are essential ordinances just as there are required courses. There are prescribed standards of worthiness. If we resist them, avoid them, or fail them, we will not enter in with those who complete the course." ("The Only True Church," *Ensign,* November 1985, 82)

There is only one priesthood, but there are two divisions within it that our Father in Heaven shares with us on the earth:

> There are, in the church, two priesthoods, namely, the Melchizedek and Aaronic, including the Levitical Priesthood.
>
> Why the first is called the Melchizedek Priesthood is because Melchizedek was such a great high priest.
>
> Before his day it was called *the Holy Priesthood, after the Order of the Son of God.*
>
> But out of respect or reverence to the name of the Supreme Being, to avoid the too frequent repetition of his name, they, the church, in ancient days, called that priesthood after Melchizedek, or the Melchizedek Priesthood.
>
> All other authorities or offices in the church are appendages to this priesthood.
>
> But there are two divisions or grand heads—one is the Melchizedek Priesthood, and the other is the Aaronic or Levitical Priesthood. . . .
>
> The second priesthood is called the Priesthood of Aaron, because it was conferred upon Aaron and his seed, throughout all their generations.
>
> Why it is called the lesser priesthood is because it is an appendage to the greater, or the Melchizedek Priesthood, and has power in administering outward ordinances. . . .
>
> The power and authority of the higher, or Melchizedek Priesthood, is to hold the keys of all the spiritual blessings of the church—
>
> To have the privilege of receiving the mysteries of the kingdom of heaven, to have the heavens opened unto them, to commune with the general assembly and church of the Firstborn, and to enjoy the communion and presence

> of God the Father, and Jesus the mediator of the new covenant.
>
> The power and authority of the lesser, or Aaronic Priesthood, is to hold the keys of the ministering of angels, and to administer in outward ordinances, the letter of the gospel, the baptism of repentance for the remission of sins, agreeable to the covenants and commandments. (D&C 107:1–6, 13–14, 18–20)

The higher priesthood was held by all of the ancient patriarchs and was passed down from father to son. This patriarchal order ended for the common man in Israel with the translation of Moses, although the Melchizedek Priesthood was most assuredly held by all of the Lord's prophets. From the departure of Moses on, the scriptures tell us, only one of the twelve tribes of Israel was allowed to hold the priesthood of God, and that was the tribe of Levi. This tribe held the Aaronic Priesthood, which is the lesser priesthood. This priesthood, also referred to as the Levitical Priesthood, carried with it the power and authority to administer the lesser ordinances of the gospel, namely baptism.

When the children of Israel left Egypt under the tutelage of Moses, they were led to Mount Sinai to receive the higher ordinances of our Father in Heaven. These ordinances carry with them covenants of a serious nature, and a person must therefore be prepared to live up to those higher standards before accepting them. The children of Israel were steeped in the customs of Egypt, which included the worship of idols, as evidenced by their behavior in fashioning a golden calf while Moses was on the mount communing with the Lord.

The Egyptians worshipped a multiplicity of gods and would seek to supplicate the favors of whichever god they needed for their predicament at any given time. It would appear that Jehovah had fit very nicely into Israel's pantheon as their "god of war":

> Thus the Lord saved Israel that day out of the hand of the Egyptians; and Israel saw the Egyptians dead upon the sea shore.
>
> And Israel saw that great work which the

Lord did upon the Egyptians: and the people feared the Lord, and believed the Lord, and his servant Moses.

Then sang Moses and the children of Israel this song unto the Lord, and spake, saying, I will sing unto the Lord, for he hath triumphed gloriously: the horse and his rider hath he thrown into the sea.

The Lord is my strength and song, and he is become my salvation: he is my God, and I will prepare him an habitation; my father's God, and I will exalt him.

The Lord is a man of war: the Lord is his name.

Pharaoh's chariots and his host hath he cast into the sea: his chosen captains also are drowned in the Red sea.

The depths have covered them: they sank into the bottom as a stone.

Thy right hand, O Lord, is become glorious in power: thy right hand, O Lord, hath dashed in pieces the enemy.

And in the greatness of thine excellency thou hast overthrown them that rose up against thee: thou sentest forth thy wrath, which consumed them as stubble.

And with the blast of thy nostrils the waters were gathered together, the floods stood upright as an heap, and the depths were congealed in the heart of the sea.

The enemy said, I will pursue, I will overtake, I will divide the spoil; my lust shall be satisfied upon them; I will draw my sword, my hand shall destroy them.

Thou didst blow with thy wind, the sea covered them: they sank as lead in the mighty waters.

Who is like unto thee, O Lord, among

> the gods? Who is like thee, glorious in holiness, fearful in praises, doing wonders? (Exodus 14:30–31; 15:1–11)

When Moses delayed his return, the children of Israel apparently went back to worshipping the particular god that the golden calf represented. This would make sense, given their lack of spiritual knowledge and maturity. If they had been permitted to enter into the higher ordinances of the Melchizedek Priesthood, it would have been, in essence, like signing their spiritual death order. With such a lack of spiritual maturity, they would have been incapable of living up to the conditions that attended those higher ordinances. In effect, they would have been damned for things that would have been beyond their control.

Our Heavenly Father desires that which is best for all of His spirit children. From what I have surmised from the scriptures concerning Him and His nature, it appears that He is a loving father, not a vengeful ruler. I am positive that He will, in the end, give us the most that He can under the eternal laws of justice and mercy. However, the fact remains that each of us must make the final decision as to what we will inherit in the eternities. Moroni recorded:

> Do ye suppose that ye shall dwell with him under a consciousness of your guilt? Do ye suppose that ye could be happy to dwell with that holy Being, when your souls are racked with a consciousness of guilt that ye have ever abused his laws?
>
> Behold, I say unto you that ye would be more miserable to dwell with a holy and just God, under a consciousness of your filthiness before him, than ye would to dwell with the damned souls in hell. (Mormon 9:3–4)

It appears that in the eternal world we will inherit the conditions in which we will be most comfortable, given our personal dispositions. Furthermore, it appears that eternal law binds our Father in Heaven regarding what eternal reward He can bestow upon us. Though He may wish He could reward us with more, eternal justice requires that each of us inherit what we have warranted through our obedience, or disobedience, to the laws of the gospel during our mortal probation. As the supreme holder of the sacred priesthood, He will execute all judgment according to the eternal laws, which govern the universe. Of this we can be assured. He will honor that sacred priesthood no matter what. If He did not, He would cease to be God, and it is that priesthood power that allows Him to be who He is.

If we have received the ordinances of the holy priesthood and have lived up to the covenants inherent in them, even though we are not yet as He is, He can bestow upon us all that He has. We all grow in this life from grace to grace. We learn line upon line, precept upon precept, here a little and there a little. It is through the obtaining and keeping of sacred covenants, many of which can only be made in the holy temple, that we can ultimately become as He is. Through this pattern and only through this pattern can we hope to obtain the salvation of God. In this way will the promise of God to the ancient patriarch Abraham find its fulfillment—that through him and his seed all of the families of the earth will be blessed.

Because of His loving nature, the Savior wants what is best for each of us. During his ministry He promised this priesthood authority to Peter and later to the rest of the Twelve: "I will give unto thee the keys of the kingdom of heaven: and whatsoever thou shalt bind on earth shall be bound in heaven: and whatsoever thou shalt loose on earth shall be loosed in heaven" (Matthew 16:19).

Covenant making is serious business, and the Lord will not be mocked (D&C 63:57–58). Where much is given by our Father or the Savior, much will be required at our hands in return (D&C 82:3). Regarding the incident involving the worshipping of the golden calf, when it seemed that Moses was not going to return from communing with the God of Abraham, Isaac, and Jacob on the mountain, the children of Israel returned to what they knew best from before their delivery from bondage:

> In the third month, when the children of Israel were gone forth out of the land of Egypt, the same day came they into the wilderness of Sinai.

For they were departed from Rephidim, and were come to the desert of Sinai, and had pitched in the wilderness; and there Israel camped before the mount.

And Moses went up unto God, and the Lord called unto him out of the mountain, saying, Thus shalt thou say to the house of Jacob, and tell the children of Israel;

Ye have seen what I did unto the Egyptians, and how I bare you on eagles' wings, and brought you unto myself.

Now therefore, if ye will obey my voice indeed, and keep my covenant, then ye shall be a peculiar treasure unto me above all people: for all the earth is mine:

And ye shall be unto me a kingdom of priests, and an holy nation. These are the words which thou shalt speak unto the children of Israel.

And Moses came and called for the elders of the people, and laid before their faces all these words which the Lord commanded him.

And all the people answered together, and said, All that the Lord hath spoken we will do. And Moses returned the words of the people unto the Lord.

And the Lord said unto Moses, Lo, I come unto thee in a thick cloud, that the people may hear when I speak with thee, and believe thee for ever. And Moses told the words of the people unto the Lord.

And the Lord said unto Moses, Go unto the people, and sanctify them to day and to morrow, and let them wash their clothes,

And be ready against the third day: for the third day the Lord will come down in the sight of all the people upon mount Sinai. (Exodus 19:1–11)

At the time the Lord gave unto Moses the Ten Commandments, the children of Israel were afraid to face God (Exodus 20:18–22). Upon his return, Moses, observing Israel's deplorable condition, returned to the mountain to see what the Lord would have him do. Instead of giving the people the ordinances of the higher priesthood, the Lord decided to give them a lesser set of laws and regulations, which they, at their level of spirituality and knowledge, could reasonably follow. This way they would not bring condemnation upon themselves by being asked to live something they were incapable of living.

> And the Lord said unto Moses, Hew thee two other tables of stone, like unto the first, and I will write upon them also, the words of the law, according as they were written at the first on the tables which thou brakest; but it shall not be according to the first, for I will take away the priesthood out of their midst; therefore my holy order, and the ordinances thereof, shall not go before them; for my presence shall not go up in their midst, lest I destroy them.
>
> But I will give unto them the law as at the first, but it shall be after the law of a carnal commandment; for I have sworn in my wrath, that they shall not enter into my presence, into my rest, in the days of their pilgrimage. Therefore do as I have commanded thee, and be ready in the morning, and come up in the morning unto mount Sinai, and present thyself there to me, in the top of the mount.
>
> And no man shall come up with thee, neither let any man be seen throughout all the mount; neither let the flocks nor herds feed before that mount. And Moses hewed two tables of stone like unto the first; and he rose up early in the morning, and went up unto mount Sinai, as the Lord had commanded him, and took in his hand the two tables of stone. (JST, Exodus 34:1–4)

Rather than looking at this alternative as a punishment, let's look at it from an eternal perspective. Should the children of Israel have been allowed to enter into the ordinances and covenants of the higher (Melchizedek) priesthood in their vacillating condition, they would of necessity have been required to live up to stringent requirements that were beyond their current capacity.

Thus, the law of Moses became a schoolmaster to ancient Israel. It was in essence a set of conditions to prepare them for the higher ordinances and covenants that Christ Himself would bring when He made His mortal advent in the meridian of time. Jesus told the Jews that the lesser law was fulfilled in Him because He had come in the flesh to institute the higher law. He explained that He was not destroying the law, nor the teachings of the former prophets, but rather that the very purpose of the law, to prepare Israel for His advent, had come to fruition in Him (Matthew 5:17–18). Those higher ordinances and covenants would be those of the Melchizedek Priesthood, which He held and which He would once again make available to the common man. The higher priesthood contained the ordinances required to attain salvation. Without these ordinances, salvation is not attainable. Thus, we receive counsel in Hebrews 7 on the necessity of obtaining both priesthoods:

> If therefore perfection were by the Levitical priesthood, (for under it the people received the law,) what further need was there that another priest should rise after the order of Melchisedec, and not be called after the order of Aaron?
>
> For the priesthood being changed, there is made of necessity a change also of the law. (Hebrews 7:11–12)

The Savior similarly desires for latter-day Israel to be endowed with His power from on high:

> For, for this cause I commanded Moses that he should build a tabernacle, that they should bear it with them in the wilderness, and to build a house in the land of promise, that those ordi-

> nances might be revealed which had been hid from before the world was.
>
> Therefore, verily I say unto you, that your anointings, and your washings, and your baptisms for the dead, and your solemn assemblies, and your memorials for your sacrifices by the sons of Levi, and for your oracles in your most holy places wherein you receive conversations, and your statutes and judgments, for the beginning of the revelations and foundation of Zion, and for the glory, honor, and endowment of all her municipals, are ordained by the ordinance of my holy house, which my people are always commanded to build unto my holy name.
>
> And verily I say unto you, let this house be built unto my name, that I may reveal mine ordinances therein unto my people;
>
> For I deign to reveal unto my church things which have been kept hid from before the foundation of the world, things that pertain to the dispensation of the fulness of times. (D&C 124:38–41)

Many have felt shunned or discriminated against by members of The Church of Jesus Christ of Latter-day Saints because they cannot enter into the holy temples that dot the earth. But not even members of the Church can enter into these sacred temples without passing a stringent interview to receive a temple recommend. If the Church is, as we claim, the kingdom of God on the earth, then things are as our Savior would have them. If not, then the world is not really missing out on anything because we don't truly have the priesthood of God.

Bearers of the Aaronic Priesthood can perform the ordinance of baptism. They can also administer the emblems of the sacrament of the Lord's Supper. But that is the extent of the ordinances of the lesser, or Levitical priesthood. The ordinances of the Aaronic Priesthood constitute the gate through which all must pass to enter the strait and narrow path leading to eternal life. Through them we receive the condition of justification, discussed in chapter five. For us to gain salvation to the fullest extent, we must obtain the ordinances of the Melchizedek Priesthood. Those ordinances are obtained only within the sacred walls of the aforementioned holy temples. It is the ordinances of the temple that provide the path leading to exaltation. It is through them that we can reach the state of sanctification. This is the reason for Paul's teachings in Hebrews 7.

Marriages solemnized within the holy temple have the possibility of becoming eternal in nature. Latter-day Saint doctrine stipulates that "nevertheless neither is the man without the woman, neither the woman without the man, in the Lord. For as the woman is of the man, even so is the man also by the woman; but all things of God" (1 Corinthians 11:11–12).

The Doctrine and Covenants clarifies this doctrine further:

> In the celestial glory there are three heavens or degrees; and in order to obtain the highest, a man must enter into this order of the priesthood [meaning the new and everlasting covenant of marriage];
>
> And if he does not, he cannot obtain it. He may enter into the other, but that is the end of his kingdom; he cannot have an increase. . . .
>
> The more sure word of prophecy means a man's knowing that he is sealed up unto eternal life, by revelation and the spirit of prophecy, through the power of the Holy Priesthood. (D&C 131:1–5)

As we can see, temple marriage is the major prerequisite for obtaining eternal life. However, according to the Apostle Paul, obtaining the two priesthoods is required to gain salvation. So what is the status of women, who don't hold the priesthood of God? Herein lies the beauty of the marvelous plan of our Father in Heaven. Just as we become the sons and daughters of Christ (part of His family) when we are baptized, so also does the wife share in the priesthood of her husband as they become one in the sealing ordinance of the temple. She can become sanctified through his priesthood.

Our Father in Heaven has chosen to share two main powers of Godhood with His spirit children here in mortality. If He lacked either of these powers, He could not be God. One of them is His priesthood, which is held by the man. The other power is the ability to bring forth life, which is the role of the woman. With this in mind, it should not be too difficult to see how the marvelous plan of the Father finds fulfillment through marriage. No man can be exalted by himself because he cannot by himself create offspring. No woman can be exalted by herself because she cannot hold the priesthood.

I recall hearing someone explain it this way: "Our Heavenly Father let women bear children, so as a consolation prize He gave men the priesthood." I like this way of summarizing the sacred role of creating offspring. This statement was not made flippantly, and in citing it I'm not trying to lessen the importance of the priesthood but rather to elevate the crucial role of women in bearing and rearing children. The priesthood is the power by which the earth and everything on it were created—the power by which the Savior and His apostles healed the sick, gave sight to the blind, made the lame to walk, and raised the dead. It was this sacred power that allowed Him to rise from the grave on the third day, thus conquering death. And it is this same priesthood power that will someday, through the saving grace of the Atonement, raise each of us from our own mortal graves to immortality. Likewise, it is through power from God that the woman can conceive and bear children. Without either of these essential powers, our Heavenly Father could not be God. Both of these powers are necessary for Him to be who He is.

When one considers all of the saving ordinances that a loving Father in Heaven has given to man to help him progress toward exaltation, the inadequacies of the doctrine of being saved by grace (as most of the Christian world perceives it) becomes evident. Belief alone just simply will not qualify a soul for salvation, any more than a woman can hold the priesthood or a man can conceive and bear offspring. The world, therefore, needs to know and understand the doctrine of celestial marriage, as well as the other saving ordinances so they can obtain these proper ordinances of salvation from authorized servants of the Lord Jesus Christ.

We were all sent to this mortal existence to gain the experiences necessary to become like our Heavenly Father. Isn't it marvelous that He has shared these two sacred powers of Godhood with us to help us in our progression toward that goal? This doctrine is not a new one. A modern-day prophet, President Howard W. Hunter said that there are prerequisites to obtaining eternal life:

> If keeping the commandments is a prerequisite to the obtaining of eternal life, then some of the things that a man must do are as follows:
>
> 1. Have a belief in Jesus Christ and accept the principles of his gospel.
>
> 2. Be baptized, receive the Holy Ghost, and live to be worthy of his companionship.
>
> 3. Receive the Melchizedek Priesthood, magnify an assigned office therein, and merit this promise of the Lord—"All that my Father hath shall be given unto him." (D&C 84:38)
>
> 4. Enter into and keep the new and everlasting covenant of marriage.
>
> 5. Keep all the commandments and endure to the end.
>
> One of the purposes of this mortal life is to give us the opportunity to prepare to meet God and go on with him in eternal life by living the fullness of the gospel law. (Hunter, *Teachings of Howard W. Hunter,* 24.)

Other modern-day Church leaders have commented on the place of the ordinances of the holy priesthood in our eternal progression. President Gordon B. Hinckley said:

> These unique and wonderful buildings, and the ordinances administered therein, represent the ultimate in our worship. These ordinances become the most profound expressions of our theology. I urge our people everywhere . . . to live worthy to hold a temple recommend, to secure one and regard it as a precious asset, and to make

> a greater effort to go to the house of the Lord and partake of the spirit and blessings to be had therein. ("Of Missions, Temples, and Stewardship," *Ensign,* November 1995, 53).

President Boyd K. Packer declared:

> The ordinances and ceremonies of the temple are simple. They are beautiful. They are sacred. They are kept confidential lest they be given to those who are unprepared. Curiosity is not a preparation. Deep interest itself is not a preparation. Preparation for the ordinances include preliminary steps: faith, repentance, baptism, confirmation, worthiness, a maturity and dignity worthy of one who comes invited as a guest into the house of the Lord. ("The Holy Temple," *Ensign,* February 1995, 32)

Elder Russell M. Nelson taught:

> There are two concepts we especially need to keep in mind as we prepare for the temple. The first is covenant. We need to remember that a covenant is a promise. A covenant made with God should be regarded not as restrictive, but as protective. Covenants with Him protect us from danger. . . .
>
> The second concept to stress in our mental preparation is Atonement. The Atonement of Jesus Christ is the central act of all human history. It is the core of the plan of salvation. Without the infinite Atonement, all mankind would be irretrievably lost. Temple ordinances and covenants teach of the redeeming power of the Atonement.
>
> Brothers and sisters, Christ paid such an enormous, enabling price for us! Will we not

> apply His Atonement in order to pay the much smaller price required for personal progress? (see Mosiah 4:2). Being valiant in our testimony of Jesus, therefore, includes being valiant in our efforts to live more as He lived (see D&C 76:79). We certainly cannot enter His kingdom without receiving the restored ordinances and keeping their associated covenants, but neither can we enter His kingdom without having significantly developed our charity and the other cardinal attributes (see Ether 12:34). Yes, we need the essential ordinances, but we also need the essential attributes. Yes, we need to keep our covenants, but we also need to develop our character. ("Prepare for Blessings of the Temple," *Ensign,* March 2002, 21–22)

According to the prophet Nephi, when the Bible was originally penned it contained the teachings concerning these ordinances, along with many other doctrines. They were explained in simple terms that were easy to understand. But many of these plain and precious truths have been lost through retranslation, as well as being intentionally taken out of the Holy Scriptures by evil men. This has resulted in countless numbers of people stumbling and subsequently not receiving necessary ordinances because of misconceptions and false interpretations (1 Nephi 13:20–29).

It should be evident from this chapter that salvation comes though membership in Christ's church. The first chapter of 1 Corinthians contains a scathing rebuke from the Apostle Paul to the members of the Church at Corinth. Many of these Jewish proselytes had begun to fall away from the Church and its teachings and to align themselves with certain splinter groups of the day.

The Apostle Paul rebuked the Saints for putting their trust in the words and teachings of men instead of in the words of the Savior. Elder Mark E. Petersen commented on this reprimand:

> When the Savior established his church

during his mortal ministry, and as it was further developed by the twelve apostles of that day, one important fact became conspicuously clear, which is: that salvation comes through the Church.

It does not come through any separate organization or splinter group nor to any private party as an individual. It comes only through the Church itself as the Lord established it.

It was the Church that was organized for the perfecting of the Saints. It was the Church that was given for the work of the ministry. It was the Church that was provided to edify the body of Christ, as Paul explained to the Ephesians.

Therefore it was made clearly manifest that salvation is *in* the Church, and *of* the Church, and is obtained only *through* the Church.

The Lord established one strait and narrow way, and understandingly observed that "few there be that find it."

Not only did he provide that salvation should come through his regularly constituted church, but he set up safeguards to protect its members from being tossed to and fro with every wind of doctrine and to preserve them from the sleight of men who, with cunning craftiness, lie in wait to deceive. (See Ephesians 4:14.)

Those safeguards, according to Paul's epistle to the Ephesians, rested primarily in the persons of the apostles and prophets whom God placed at the head of the Church for that specific purpose.

They were the inspired leaders in the Church. They were the mouthpieces of the Lord, and their inspired messages to the people were the will of the Lord, the mind of the Lord, the voice of the Lord, and the power of God unto salvation. (See D&C 68:4.)

With such heavenly guidance, none need go

> astray. ("Salvation Comes through the Church," *Ensign*, July 1973, 108)

The same holds true for us in this day. Without the blessings of membership in the Church, salvation in the fullest sense is not available to us. Just being a member of the Church is not enough either. We must be active, vibrant, living members of the faith if we want to merit the fullness of our Fathers' kingdom. Through growing from grace to grace within the activities and ordinances, which are afforded us in His true church, we can increasingly progress toward becoming as He is. This is the purpose of the plan of our Father, and ever has been, from the beginning of mankind.

The Apostle Paul, in his parting commentary to the Saints at Caesarea Philippi, said:

> I count all things but loss for the excellency of the knowledge of Christ Jesus my Lord: for whom I have suffered the loss of all things, and do count them but dung, that I may win Christ,
>
> And be found in him, not having mine own righteousness, which is of the law, but that which is through the faith of Christ, the righteousness which is of God by faith:
>
> That I may know him, and the power of his resurrection, and the fellowship of his sufferings, being made conformable unto his death;
>
> If by any means I might attain unto the resurrection of the dead.
>
> Not as though I had already attained, either were already perfect: but I follow after, if that I may apprehend that for which also I am apprehended of Christ Jesus.
>
> Brethren, I count not myself to have apprehended: but this one thing I do, forgetting those things which are behind, and reaching forth unto those things which are before,
>
> I press toward the mark for the prize of the

> high calling of God in Christ Jesus.
>
> Let us therefore, as many as be perfect, be thus minded: and if in any thing ye be otherwise minded, God shall reveal even this unto you. (Philippians 3:9–15)

Paul was already an apostle of the Christ, one of His special witnesses. And as such he was a prophet, seer, and revelator of the Savior's calling. What higher calling would he seek?

Chapter 14

Judgment and Eternal Inheritance

The spirit and the body shall be reunited again in its perfect form; both limb and joint shall be restored to its proper frame, even as we now are at this time; and we shall be brought to stand before God, knowing even as we know now, and have a bright recollection of all our guilt.

Now, this restoration shall come to all, both old and young, both bond and free, both male and female, both the wicked and the righteous; and even there shall not so much as a hair of their heads be lost; but every thing shall be restored to its perfect frame, as it is now, or in the body, and shall be brought and be arraigned before the bar of Christ the Son, and God the Father, and the Holy Spirit, which is one Eternal God, to be judged according to their works, whether they be good or whether they be evil.

—Alma 11:43–44

I recently spent a few days with a boyhood friend whom I had not seen for many years. We reminisced until the wee hours of the morning about the experiences of our youth. One particular experience stood out in my mind as we conversed that night.

When we were in the fifth grade, my athletic prowess taught me a valuable lesson in the area of obedience. Our school building was U-shaped, with classrooms surrounding a grassy courtyard. In our school, the eleventh commandment was, "Thou shalt not play ball in the inner courtyard of the school grounds." The object of the directive was to keep glass in all of the window frames of the classrooms. It just so happened one day that we, along with another of our buddies, somehow ended up standing in that inner sanctuary with a football in our hands. Against our better judgment we began to throw it and kick it back and forth. I recall my buddies advising me that we had better cease our frolicking and take our game to the playground, but I was sure that we wouldn't break a window. I was the local and regional punt, pass, and kick champion practically every year during my youth, but distance, not accuracy, was my forte when it came to my kicking game.

After one kick, I knew as soon as the ball left my foot that our playing in the courtyard had been a bad idea. As I watched the ball's trajectory, everything seemed to happen in slow motion. In football terms, my punt would be called a shank. It arched majestically toward the largest window in our classroom. The sound of shattering glass was horrible. All I could think of was how many years worth of allowances it was going to take me to pay for my disobedience. The replacement cost of the window ended up coming out of all of our parents' pockets, so the sting wasn't quite so bad—though my friends' parents weren't too excited about the prospect of their sons playing ball with me in the future!

Looking back on that experience, I can still recall how scared and regretful I felt for not being more obedient to the rules. At the time, I would have given just about anything to have the chance to go back and do things differently. The sad truth is that once we have committed an act, we can't go back and undo it. The longer I live, the more I see the wisdom and truth in a number of the Lord's statements:

> There is a law, irrevocably decreed in heaven before the foundations of this world, upon

> which all blessings are predicated—and when we obtain any blessing from God, it is by obedience to that law upon which it is predicated. (D&C 130:20–21)
>
> For behold, I reveal unto you a new and an everlasting covenant; and if ye abide not that covenant, then are ye damned; for no one can reject this covenant and be permitted to enter into my glory.
>
> For all who will have a blessing at my hands shall abide the law which was appointed for that blessing, and the conditions thereof, as were instituted from before the foundation of the world.
>
> And as pertaining to the new and everlasting covenant, it was instituted for the fullness of my glory; and he that receiveth a fulness thereof must and shall abide the law, or he shall be damned, saith the Lord God.
>
> And verily I say unto you, that the conditions of this law are these: All covenants, contracts, bonds, obligations, oaths, vows, performances, connections, associations, or expectations, that are not made and entered into and sealed by the Holy Spirit of promise, of him who is anointed, both as well for time and for all eternity, and that too most holy, by revelation and commandment through the medium of mine anointed, whom I have appointed on the earth to hold this power, . . . are of no efficacy, virtue, or force in and after the resurrection from the dead. (D&C 132:4–7)

It is apparent that the Lord isn't kidding around when it comes to the principles pertaining to the salvation of mankind. Another scripture casts further illumination on this critical doctrine: "It is impossible for a man to be saved in ignorance" (D&C 131:6).

I have met many people over the years who have accused Latter-day

Saints of pompous arrogance. They have perceived that we are saying to the rest of the world, "If you don't join our church, you will burn in hell." First of all, The Church of Jesus Christ of Latter-day Saints is not anyone's church but His whose name it bears, the God who gave us commandments and then came to earth and subjected Himself to mortality so that we might live again. That truth casts a little different light on what we are really saying to the world. Does one need to be a Mormon to be saved? The answer to that question is no. In reality, there is no such thing as a Mormon. Must individuals align themselves with Christ's church if they wish to obtain salvation? Most definitely!

All we are simply saying is that this is the Church of Jesus Christ . . . of Latter-day Saints. We have been blessed to be able to belong to it and be numbered with the saints of God in these last days. The Savior desires that all of us become His spiritual sons and daughters, entering into covenants that will allow His atonement to cover our many sins and transgressions. If this truly is His church, then we must align ourselves with it if we expect to be able to regain His presence.

We all must be given the opportunity to hear the truths of Christ's glorious gospel. We will then of our own free will and choice be given the opportunity to either accept or reject the gospel message.

Those who choose to enter into a covenant with their Savior through baptism by a duly authorized servant holding His priesthood will then be confirmed a member of His church. They become the elect of God and will be numbered with the Saints of God, becoming eligible for the other saving ordinances of the Savior's gospel, which are correctly offered only in His church (see chapter thirteen). Those who have died without hearing His gospel will be given the opportunity to accept it (1 Peter 3:18–21). They will then be judged according to the flesh (mortality). In other words, they will be judged the same as if they had heard and accepted it while still in mortality (1 Peter 4:6). This is in accordance with the equity of a just God who desires all, but will force none, to follow Him.

We are told in the scriptures that our judgment will ultimately be meted out by the Savior of this world (John 5:21–22; 2 Nephi 9:41). The conditions surrounding our afterlife are probably the most important, yet least understood, of any of the mysteries of our Father in Heaven. What happens to a person when he dies? Is that the end? Do those of us who do evil in this life go to a place of fire and brimstone where a little red guy with horns, a tail, and a pitchfork will be waiting to greet us and exile us to an eternity of hell? Do those of us who have passed our test of mortality become angels with wings and just float around for eternity playing a harp? I sincerely hope not! If anyone had to endure my harp playing, it wouldn't take long for them to think that they weren't in heaven.

We all need to understand the definitions of both heaven and hell. When individuals die, a partial judgment occurs immediately, whereby they enter the world of spirits into either a condition known as paradise or a condition referred to as spirit prison. In his writings in the Book of Mormon, the prophet Alma has given us valuable insight into this doctrine:

> Now, concerning the state of the soul between death and the resurrection—behold, it has been made known unto me by an angel, that the spirits of all men, as soon as they are departed from this mortal body, yea, the spirits of all men, whether they be good or evil, are taken home to that God who gave them life.
>
> And then shall it come to pass, that the spirits of those who are righteous are received into a state of happiness, which is called paradise, a state of rest, a state of peace, where they shall rest from all their troubles and from all care, and sorrow.
>
> And then shall it come to pass, that the spirits of the wicked, yea, who are evil—for behold, they have no part nor portion of the Spirit of the Lord; for behold, they chose evil works rather than good; therefore the spirit of the devil did enter into them, and take possession of their house—and these shall be cast out into outer darkness; there shall be weeping, and wailing, and gnashing of teeth, and this because of their own iniquity, being led captive by the will of the devil.

> Now this is the state of the souls of the wicked, yea, in darkness, and a state of awful, fearful looking for the fiery indignation of the wrath of God upon them; thus they remain in this state, as well as the righteous in paradise, until the time of their resurrection. (Alma 40:11–14)

Ponder this statement, if you will, from the *Encyclopedia of Mormonism:*

> LDS eschatology also offers several distinct doctrines. For example, Latter-day Saints believe in a temporary state between death and resurrection that the scriptures call the spirit world. This temporary spirit world includes Paradise, where the spirits of the righteous await their glorious resurrection, and Hell, where the spirits of the wicked suffer for their sins while they await resurrection to a lesser degree of glory (Alma 40:11–14; cf. Luke 16:22–23). LDS doctrine teaches that every human being will be resurrected. Many were resurrected soon after Jesus' resurrection; the remaining righteous will be resurrected at the second coming of Christ, and the wicked at the end of Christ's one-thousand-year reign on earth. Hell is a temporary condition, which will yield up its captive spirits at the Resurrection, just as death will yield up its bodies (2 Nephi 9:10–14; cf. Revelation 20:13–14). In the Resurrection all suffering comes to an end (D&C 76:84, 88–89), and all human beings except the sons of perdition will be saved in one of the three kingdoms, or degrees of glory: the celestial, the terrestrial, or the telestial (D&C 76:1–19; 88:29–32; cf. 1 Corinthians 15:4–42). (*Encyclopedia of Mormonism,* 398)

President Joseph F. Smith discussed this subject further:

> The spirits of all men, as soon as they depart from this mortal body, whether they are good or evil . . . are taken home to that God who gave them life, where there is a separation, a partial judgment, and the spirits of those who are righteous are received into a state of happiness which is called paradise, a state of rest, a state of peace, where they expand in wisdom, where they have respite from all their troubles, and where care and sorrow do not annoy. The wicked, on the contrary, have no part nor portion in the Spirit of the Lord, and they are cast into outer darkness, being led captive, because of their own iniquity, by the evil one. And in this space between death and the resurrection of the body, the two classes of souls remain, in happiness or in misery, until the time which is appointed of God that the dead shall come forth and be reunited both spirit and body, and be brought to stand before God, and be judged according to their works. This is the final judgment. (*Gospel Doctrine,* 448).

President Brigham Young declared:

> When you lay down this tabernacle, where are you going? Into the spiritual world. . . . Where is the spirit world? It is right here. Do the good and evil spirits go together? Yes they do. . . . Do they go beyond the boundaries of the organized earth? No, they do not. . . . Can you see it with your natural eyes? No. Can you see spirits in this room? No. Suppose the Lord should touch your eyes that you might see, could you then see the spirits? Yes, as plainly as you now see bodies. (Widtsoe, *Discourses of Brigham Young,* 376–77)

Hell, or Outer Darkness

Another term for this condition into which the wicked are cast is hell. The full effect of Christ's atonement will cover only those who accept the Savior, entering into the aforementioned covenants with Him through membership in His church. Those who reject His gift of grace will be cast into hell between death and their resurrection. There they will pay the price required to atone for their sins. When they have paid sufficiently for their disobedience and have learned to be obedient to the laws they chose not to live in mortality, they will be allowed to come out of hell. Only then will they be prepared to inherit a degree of our Heavenly Father's glory, which He has prepared for them.

One group wanted no part of our Father's plan or its inherent glory. These are referred to in the scriptures as "sons of perdition" and will, at the end of the Millennium, be cast into outer darkness forever to dwell with Satan as his children. "For they love darkness rather than light, and their deeds are evil, and they receive their wages of whom they list to obey," but where the Father and the Son dwell, they cannot come, for there is no forgiveness for them in this world nor in the world to come (D&C 29:45; 76:26, 32, 34).

"And another trump shall sound, which is the fourth trump, saying: There are found among those who are to remain until that great and last day, even the end, who shall remain filthy still" (D&C 88:102).

This condition of outer darkness will be so miserable that the Father has not seen fit to reveal details concerning that existence. While we do not fully understand either what it will be like in hell, the Savior has given us a significant amount of insight into the type of experience it will be:

> I, having accomplished and finished the will of him whose I am, even the Father, concerning me—having done this that I might subdue all things unto myself—
>
> Retaining all power, even to the destroying of Satan and his works at the end of the world, and the last great day of judgment, which I shall

> pass upon the inhabitants thereof, judging every man according to his works and the deeds which he hath done.
>
> And surely every man must repent or suffer, for I, God, am endless. Wherefore, I revoke not the judgments which I shall pass, but woes shall go forth, weeping, wailing and gnashing of teeth, yea, to those who are found on my left hand.
>
> Nevertheless, it is not written that there shall be no end to this torment, but it is written *endless torment.*
>
> Again, it is written *eternal damnation;* wherefore it is more express than other scriptures, that it might work upon the hearts of the children of men, altogether for my name's glory.
>
> Wherefore, I will explain unto you this mystery, for it is meet unto you to know even as mine apostles. I speak unto you that are chosen in this thing, even as one, that you may enter into my rest.
>
> For, behold, the mystery of godliness, how great is it! For, behold, I am endless, and the punishment which is given from my hand is endless punishment, for Endless is my name. Wherefore—
>
> Eternal punishment is God's punishment. Endless punishment is God's punishment. (D&C 19:2–11)

The doctrines of The Church of Jesus Christ of Latter-day Saints concerning man's conditions in the afterlife separate it from every other Christian religion upon the face of the earth. From modern-day scripture, we learn that hell has an end (except for the sons of perdition, who will be cast back into it for eternity). These verses also introduce another interesting doctrine, which is why the scriptures refer to hell as endless and eternal, even though it will not continue forever.

In the writings of the prophet Isaiah we are given a few of the many names by which our Savior, Jesus Christ, would be known: "For unto us a child is born, unto us a son is given: and the government shall be upon his shoulder: and his name shall be called Wonderful, Counselor, The mighty God, The everlasting Father, The Prince of Peace" (Isaiah 9:6). Many more names are used in the scriptures in reference to the Savior, including Jehovah, the Messiah, Lamb of God, Good Shepherd, Son of God, the Great I Am, Marvelous, the Light of the World, Living Water, Bread of Life, Endless, and Eternal.

Let us focus on the final two names cited: Endless and Eternal. It seems that while most of the Christian world assumes one thing about hell, the Lord is actually saying something quite different. Endless punishment, or eternal punishment, is God's punishment. We return to the Doctrine and Covenants for a more in-depth study of hell:

> Therefore I command you to repent—repent, lest I smite you by the rod of my mouth, and by my wrath, and by my anger, and your sufferings be sore—how sore you know not, how exquisite you know not, yea, how hard to bear you know not.
>
> For behold, I, God, have suffered these things for all, that they might not suffer if they would repent; but if they would not repent they must suffer even as I;
>
> Which suffering caused myself, even God, the greatest of all, to tremble because of pain, and to bleed at every pore, and to suffer both body and spirit—and would that I might not drink the bitter cup, and shrink—
>
> Wherefore, I command you again to repent, lest I humble you with my almighty power; and that you confess your sins, lest you suffer these punishments of which I have spoken, of which in the smallest, yea, even in the least degree you have tasted at the time I withdrew my Spirit. (D&C 19:15–18, 20)

Talk about insight! In these few verses the Savior gives us a glimpse of what he had to endure to execute the greatest event in the history of the universe—His atonement. He also gives us an insight into how horrible the pains of hell will be for those who do not repent:

> And while we were yet in the Spirit, the Lord commanded us that we should write the vision; for we beheld Satan, that old serpent, even the devil, who rebelled against God, and sought to take the kingdom of our God and his Christ—
>
> Wherefore, he maketh war with the saints of God, and encompasseth them round about.
>
> And we saw a vision of the sufferings of those with whom he made war and overcame, for thus came the voice of the Lord unto us:
>
> Thus saith the Lord concerning all those who know my power, and have been made partakers thereof, and suffered themselves through the power of the devil to be overcome, and to deny the truth and defy my power—
>
> They are they who are the sons of perdition, of whom I say that it had been better for them never to have been born;
>
> For they are vessels of wrath, doomed to suffer the wrath of God, with the devil and his angels in eternity;
>
> Concerning whom I have said there is no forgiveness in this world nor in the world to come—
>
> Having denied the Holy Spirit after having received it, and having denied the Only Begotten Son of the Father, having crucified him unto themselves and put him to an open shame.
>
> These are they who shall go away into the lake of fire and brimstone, with the devil and his angels—and the only ones on whom the second death shall have any power;

> Yea, verily, the only ones who shall not be redeemed in the due time of the Lord, after the sufferings of his wrath. . . .
>
> Wherefore, he saves all except them—they shall go away into everlasting punishment, which is endless punishment, which is eternal punishment, to reign with the devil and his angels in eternity, where their worm dieth not, and the fire is not quenched, which is their torment—
>
> And the end thereof, neither the place thereof, nor their torment, no man knows;
>
> Neither was it revealed, neither is, neither will be revealed unto man, except to them who are made partakers thereof;
>
> Nevertheless, I, the Lord, show it by vision unto many, but straightway shut it up again;
>
> Wherefore, the end, the width, the height, the depth, and the misery thereof, they understand not, neither any man except those who are ordained unto this condemnation.
>
> And we heard the voice, saying: Write the vision, for lo, this is the end of the vision of the sufferings of the ungodly. (D&C 76:28–38, 44–49)

The Telestial Kingdom

Those who do not qualify for either the celestial or the terrestrial kingdom will pass through hell to pay the price for their own sins. They cannot be allowed to dwell in any degree of glory until they are able to abide by the laws and conditions of that particular kingdom.

> And they who are not sanctified through the law which I have given unto you, even the law of Christ, must inherit another kingdom, even that of a terrestrial kingdom, or that of a teles-

> tial kingdom. For he who is not able to abide the law of a celestial kingdom cannot abide a celestial glory.
>
> And he who cannot abide the law of a terrestrial kingdom cannot abide a terrestrial glory.
>
> And he who cannot abide the law of a telestial kingdom cannot abide a telestial glory; therefore he is not meet for a kingdom of glory. Therefore he must abide a kingdom which is not a kingdom of glory. (D&C 88:21–24)

If we haven't learned to be obedient to even telestial laws, we will have a thousand years during the Millennium with Satan as our teacher to master obedience:

> And again, verily I say unto you, that which is governed by law is also preserved by law and perfected and sanctified by the same.
>
> That which breaketh a law, and abideth not by law, but seeketh to become a law unto itself, and willeth to abide in sin, and altogether abideth in sin, cannot be sanctified by law, neither by mercy, justice, nor judgment. Therefore, they must remain filthy still.
>
> All kingdoms have a law given; and there are many kingdoms; for there is no space in the which there is no kingdom; and there is no kingdom in which there is no space, either a greater or a lesser kingdom.
>
> And unto every kingdom is given a law; and unto every law there are certain bounds also and conditions.
>
> All beings who abide not in those conditions are not justified. (D&C 88:34–39)

At the conclusion of the thousand years, all those who are worthy of a telestial glory and have now learned to live the laws of a telestial existence, will be allowed to come forth in the Second Resurrection. At that time, they will be allowed to enter into a telestial glory. These souls will undoubtedly wish they could have inherited a greater degree of glory, but the fact will remain that they are not the kind of people who would be comfortable living in those higher conditions and living with beings who are not as they are.

> Behold, will ye believe in the day of your visitation—behold, when the Lord shall come, yea, even that great day when the earth shall be rolled together as a scroll, and the elements shall melt with fervent heat, yea, in that great day when ye shall be brought to stand before the Lamb of God—then will ye say that there is no God?
>
> Then will ye longer deny the Christ, or can ye behold the Lamb of God? Do ye suppose that ye shall dwell with him under a consciousness of your guilt? Do ye suppose that ye could be happy to dwell with that holy Being, when your souls are racked with a consciousness of guilt that ye have ever abused his laws?
>
> Behold, I say unto you that ye would be more miserable to dwell with a holy and just God, under a consciousness of your filthiness before him, than ye would to dwell with the damned souls in hell.
>
> For behold, when ye shall be brought to see your nakedness before God, and also the glory of God, and the holiness of Jesus Christ, it will kindle a flame of unquenchable fire upon you. (Mormon 9:2–5)

> And also they who are quickened by a portion of the telestial glory shall then receive of the same, even a fulness.
>
> And they who remain shall also be quickened; nevertheless, they shall return again to

> their own place, to enjoy that which they are willing to receive, because they were not willing to enjoy that which they might have received. (D&C 88:31–32.)

What a sad commentary! They could have had a fullness of their Father's glory if it had been more of a priority to them in mortality, but as the prophet Alma informs us:

> And now, my brethren, I would that, after ye have received so many witnesses, seeing that the holy scriptures testify of these things, ye come forth and bring fruit unto repentance.
>
> Yea, I would that ye would come forth and harden not your hearts any longer; for behold, now is the time and the day of your salvation; and therefore, if ye will repent and harden not your hearts, immediately shall the great plan of redemption be brought about unto you.
>
> For behold, this life is the time for men to prepare to meet God; yea, behold the day of this life is the day for men to perform their labors.
>
> And now, as I said unto you before, as ye have had so many witnesses, therefore, I beseech of you that ye do not procrastinate the day of your repentance until the end; for after this day of life, which is given us to prepare for eternity, behold, if we do not improve our time while in this life, then cometh the night of darkness wherein there can be no labor performed.
>
> Ye cannot say, when ye are brought to that awful crisis, that I will repent, that I will return to my God. Nay, ye cannot say this; for that same spirit which doth possess your bodies at the time that ye go out of this life, that same spirit will have power to possess your body in that eternal world.
>
> For behold, if ye have procrastinated the day

> of your repentance even until death, behold, ye have become subjected to the spirit of the devil, and he doth seal you his; therefore, the Spirit of the Lord hath withdrawn from you, and hath no place in you, and the devil hath all power over you; and this is the final state of the wicked. (Alma 34:30–35)

Concerning the inheritors of the telestial kingdom, we read:

> And again, we saw the glory of the telestial, which glory is that of the lesser, even as the glory of the stars differs from that of the glory of the moon in the firmament.
>
> These are they who received not the gospel of Christ, neither the testimony of Jesus.
>
> These are they who deny not the Holy Spirit.
>
> These are they who are thrust down to hell.
>
> These are they who shall not be redeemed from the devil until the last resurrection, until the Lord, even Christ the Lamb, shall have finished his work.
>
> These are they who receive not of his fulness in the eternal world, but of the Holy Spirit through the ministration of the terrestrial;
>
> And the terrestrial through the ministration of the celestial.
>
> And also the telestial receive it of the administering of angels who are appointed to minister for them, or who are appointed to be ministering spirits for them; for they shall be heirs of salvation.
>
> And thus we saw, in the heavenly vision, the glory of the telestial, which surpasses all understanding;
>
> And no man knows it except him to whom God has revealed it. (D&C 76:81–90)

And the glory of the telestial is one, even as the glory of the stars is one; for as one star differs from another star in glory, even so differs one from another in glory in the telestial world;

For these are they who are of Paul, and of Apollos, and of Cephas. These are they who say they are some of one and some of another—some of Christ and some of John, and some of Moses, and some of Elias, and some of Esaias, and some of Isaiah, and some of Enoch;

But received not the gospel, neither the testimony of Jesus, neither the prophets, neither the everlasting covenant.

Last of all, these all are they who will not be gathered with the saints, to be caught up unto the church of the Firstborn, and received into the cloud.

These are they who are liars, and sorcerers, and adulterers, and whoremongers, and whosoever loves and makes a lie.

These are they who suffer the wrath of God on earth. These are they who suffer the vengeance of eternal fire.

These are they who are cast down to hell and suffer the wrath of Almighty God, until the fulness of times, when Christ shall have subdued all enemies under his feet, and shall have perfected his work;

When he shall deliver up the kingdom, and present it unto the Father, spotless, saying: I have overcome and have trodden the wine-press alone, even the wine-press of the fierceness of the wrath of Almighty God.

Then shall he be crowned with the crown of his glory, to sit on the throne of his power to reign forever and ever.

> But behold, and lo, we saw the glory and the inhabitants of the telestial world, that they were as innumerable as the stars in the firmament of heaven, or as the sand upon the seashore;
>
> And heard the voice of the Lord saying: These all shall bow the knee, and every tongue shall confess to him who sits upon the throne forever and ever;
>
> For they shall be judged according to their works, and every man shall receive according to his own works, his own dominion, in the mansions which are prepared;
>
> And they shall be servants of the Most High; but where God and Christ dwell they cannot come, worlds without end. (D&C 76:98–112)

> And again, another trump shall sound, which is the third trump; and then come the spirits of men who are to be judged, and are found under condemnation;
>
> And these are the rest of the dead; and they live not again until the thousand years are ended, neither again, until the end of the earth. (D&C 88:100–101)

The Terrestrial Kingdom

Many have lived or will yet live upon the earth who are good, honest people. Therefore, according to the equity of a just and merciful Father, these souls will be rewarded with a far greater degree of glory than will those who attain the ranks of the telestial kingdom. Yet these are they who also didn't accept the gospel while in the flesh, perhaps because of the false teachings and deceptions of men or because they may have deemed the requirements as too great a price. These are they who weren't valiant in the testimony of Jesus. Of them we are told: "And after this another angel shall sound, which is the second trump; and then cometh the redemption of those who are Christ's at his coming; who have received their part in that prison which is prepared for them, that they might receive the gospel, and be judged according to men in the flesh" (D&C 88:99).

> And again, we saw the terrestrial world, and behold and lo, these are they who are of the terrestrial, whose glory differs from that of the church of the Firstborn who have received the fulness of the Father, even as that of the moon differs from the sun in the firmament.
>
> Behold, these are they who died without law; and also they who are the spirits of men kept in prison, whom the Son visited, and preached the gospel unto them, that they might be judged according to men in the flesh;
>
> Who received not the testimony of Jesus in the flesh, but afterwards received it.
>
> These are they who are honorable men of the earth, who were blinded by the craftiness of men. These are they who receive of his glory, but not of his fulness.
>
> These are they who receive of the presence of the Son, but not of the fulness of the Father.
>
> Wherefore, they are bodies terrestrial, and not bodies celestial, and differ in glory as the moon differs from the sun.
>
> These are they who are not valiant in the testimony of Jesus; wherefore, they obtain not the crown over the kingdom of our God.
>
> And now this is the end of the vision which we saw of the terrestrial, that the Lord commanded us to write while we were yet in the Spirit. . . .
>
> And the terrestrial through the ministration of the celestial.
>
> And also the telestial receive it of the admin-

> istering of angels who are appointed to minister for them, or who are appointed to be ministering spirits for them; for they shall be heirs of salvation.
>
> And thus we saw, in the heavenly vision, the glory of the telestial, which surpasses all understanding;
>
> And no man knows it except him to whom God has revealed it.
>
> And thus we saw the glory of the terrestrial which excels in all things the glory of the telestial, even in glory, and in power, and in might, and in dominion. (D&C 76:71–78, 87–91)

Many people today seem blinded by the bias of uninformed or misinformed persons and therefore reject the gospel message when it is offered to them. Some who have blinded these individuals are religious clergymen, who for whatever reason have managed to convince their parishioners that if they accept the message and ordinances offered by representatives of The Church of Jesus Christ of Latter-day Saints, they will lose their salvation. If these individuals do not at some point reconsider their course, they may well be among those who qualify for terrestrial glory. They may have been good people, but they failed to heed the call when it came because of fear born of those biases.

It would also appear that many of these people could be those who are guilty of sins of omission rather than sins of commission. In other words, it wasn't necessarily the things they did but the things they failed to do that will stand between them and the blessings of the celestial kingdom. However, their eternal reward will be far greater than the reward of those who inherit the telestial kingdom.

The Celestial Kingdom

The celestial kingdom is the highest of the three kingdoms of our Father in Heaven. The Apostle Paul alluded to it:

> I knew a man in Christ above fourteen years ago, (whether in the body, I cannot tell; or whether out of the body, I cannot tell: God knoweth;) such an one caught up to the third heaven.
>
> And I knew such a man, (whether in the body, or out of the body, I cannot tell: God knoweth;)
>
> How that he was caught up into paradise, and heard unspeakable words, which it is not lawful for a man to utter. (2 Corinthians 12:2–4.)

Concerning those individuals who will inherit the celestial kingdom, the Prophet Joseph Smith recorded the following:

> And again we bear record—for we saw and heard, and this is the testimony of the gospel of Christ concerning them who shall come forth in the resurrection of the just—
>
> They are they who received the testimony of Jesus, and believed on his name and were baptized after the manner of his burial, being buried in the water in his name, and this according to the commandment which he has given—
>
> That by keeping the commandments they might be washed and cleansed from all their sins, and receive the Holy Spirit by the laying on of the hands of him who is ordained and sealed unto this power;
>
> And who overcome by faith, and are sealed by the Holy Spirit of promise, which the Father sheds forth upon all those who are just and true.
>
> They are they who are the church of the Firstborn. They are they into whose hands the Father has given all things—they are they who are priests and kings, who have received of his fulness, and of his glory;
>
> And are priests of the Most High, after the

order of Melchizedek, which was after the order of Enoch, which was after the order of the Only Begotten Son. Wherefore, as it is written, they are gods, even the sons of God—

Wherefore, all things are theirs, whether life or death, or things present, or things to come, all are theirs and they are Christ's, and Christ is God's. And they shall overcome all things.

Wherefore, let no man glory in man, but rather let him glory in God, who shall subdue all enemies under his feet.

These shall dwell in the presence of God and his Christ forever and ever.

These are they whom he shall bring with him, when he shall come in the clouds of heaven to reign on the earth over his people.

These are they who shall have part in the first resurrection. These are they who shall come forth in the resurrection of the just. These are they who are come unto Mount Zion, and unto the city of the living God, the heavenly place, the holiest of all.

These are they who have come to an innumerable company of angels, to the general assembly and church of Enoch, and of the Firstborn.

These are they whose names are written in heaven, where God and Christ are the judge of all.

These are they who are just men made perfect through Jesus the mediator of the new covenant, who wrought out this perfect atonement through the shedding of his own blood.

These are they whose bodies are celestial, whose glory is that of the sun, even the glory of God, the highest of all, whose glory the sun of the firmament is written of as being typical. . . .

And thus we saw the glory of the celestial,

> which excels in all things—where God, even the Father, reigns upon his throne forever and ever;
>
> Before whose throne all things bow in humble reverence, and give him glory forever and ever.
>
> They who dwell in his presence are the church of the Firstborn; and they see as they are seen, and know as they are known, having received of his fulness and of his grace;
>
> And he makes them equal in power, and in might, and in dominion.
>
> And the glory of the celestial is one, even as the glory of the sun is one. (D&C 76:50–70; 92–96)

> And there shall be silence in heaven for the space of half an hour; and immediately after shall the curtain of heaven be unfolded, as a scroll is unfolded after it is rolled up, and the face of the Lord shall be unveiled;
>
> And the saints that are upon the earth, who are alive, shall be quickened and be caught up to meet him.
>
> And they who have slept in their graves shall come forth, for their graves shall be opened; and they also shall be caught up to meet him in the midst of the pillar of heaven—
>
> They are Christ's, the first fruits, they who shall descend with him first, and they who are on the earth and in their graves, who are first caught up to meet him; and all this by the voice of the sounding of the trump of the angel of God. (D&C 88:95–98)

Joseph Smith adds: "The place where God resides is a great Urim and Thummim. This earth, in its sanctified and immortal state, will be made like unto crystal and will be a Urim and Thummim to the inhabitants who dwell thereon, whereby all things pertaining to an inferior kingdom, or all kingdoms of a lower order, will be manifest to those who dwell on it; and this earth will be Christ's" (D&C 130:8–9).

We gain valuable insight from the scriptures concerning what is required for us to be able to successfully survive being in God's presence. Moses saw God and spoke to him face to face, "as a man speaketh unto his friend" (Exodus 33:11).

Moses learned many great truths from speaking with the Lord. The account as recorded in the book of Exodus states, "And he said, Thou canst not see my face: for there shall no man see me, and live" (Exodus 33:20). Meanwhile, we learn from verse 11 that Moses himself did precisely that. How, then, can we discern the truth of what is shared with us here? It is virtually impossible to do it from the Bible; however, from the writings of Moses, as received by the Prophet Joseph Smith, we gain a clearer picture:

> The words of God, which he spake unto Moses at a time when Moses was caught up into an exceedingly high mountain,
>
> And he saw God face to face, and he talked with him, and the glory of God was upon Moses; therefore Moses could endure his presence.
>
> And God spake unto Moses, saying: Behold, I am the Lord God Almighty, and Endless is my name; for I am without beginning of days or end of years; and is not this endless?
>
> And, behold, thou art my son; wherefore look, and I will show thee the workmanship of mine hands; but not all, for my works are without end, and also my words, for they never cease.
>
> Wherefore, no man can behold all my works, except he behold all my glory; and no man can behold all my glory, and afterwards remain in the flesh on the earth. (Moses 1:1–5)

As that marvelous experience ended, we learn how Moses was able to abide God's presence and yet remain alive:

> And the presence of God withdrew from Moses, that his glory was not upon Moses; and Moses was left unto himself. And as he was left unto himself, he fell unto the earth.
>
> And it came to pass that it was for the space of many hours before Moses did again receive his natural strength like unto man; and he said unto himself: Now, for this cause I know that man is nothing, which thing I never had supposed.
>
> But now mine own eyes have beheld God; but not my natural, but my spiritual eyes, for my natural eyes could not have beheld; for I should have withered and died in his presence; but his glory was upon me; and I beheld his face, for I was transfigured before him. (Moses 1:9–11)

It is in this final verse that Moses spells out the key part of the doctrine for us. He simply says that he was transfigured before the Lord. Immediately after this glorious experience from heaven, Satan the archdeceiver appears to Moses:

> And it came to pass that when Moses had said these words, behold, Satan came tempting him, saying: Moses, son of man, worship me.
>
> And it came to pass that Moses looked upon Satan and said: Who art thou? For behold, I am a son of God, in the similitude of his Only Begotten; and where is thy glory, that I should worship thee?
>
> For behold, I could not look upon God, except his glory should come upon me, and I were transfigured before him. But I can look upon thee in the natural man. Is it not so, surely?
>
> Blessed be the name of my God, for his Spirit hath not altogether withdrawn from me, or else where is thy glory, for it is darkness unto me? And I can judge between thee and God; for God said

> unto me: Worship God, for him only shalt thou serve. Get thee hence, Satan; deceive me not; for God said unto me: Thou art after the similitude of mine Only Begotten.
>
> And he also gave me commandments when he called unto me out of the burning bush, saying: Call upon God in the name of mine Only Begotten, and worship me.
>
> And again Moses said: I will not cease to call upon God, I have other things to inquire of him: for his glory has been upon me, wherefore I can judge between him and thee. Depart hence, Satan.
>
> And now, when Moses had said these words, Satan cried with a loud voice, and ranted upon the earth, and commanded, saying: I am the Only Begotten, worship me.
>
> And it came to pass that Moses began to fear exceedingly; and as he began to fear, he saw the bitterness of hell. Nevertheless, calling upon God, he received strength, and he commanded, saying: Depart from me, Satan, for this one God only will I worship, which is the God of glory.
>
> And now Satan began to tremble, and the earth shook; and Moses received strength, and called upon God, saying: In the name of the Only Begotten, depart hence, Satan.
>
> And it came to pass that Satan cried with a loud voice, with weeping, and wailing, and gnashing of teeth; and he departed hence, even from the presence of Moses, that he beheld him not. (Moses 1:12–22)

From this account, notice what allowed Moses to recognize that he was not in the Lord's presence. Moses could look upon his visitor with his natural eyes, or in other words, he didn't need to be transfigured to be in his presence. Many have used the passage in Exodus to support their claim that Joseph Smith couldn't have truly seen God the Father and Jesus Christ and remained alive on the earth, but here we get the criteria for such an occurrence to take place. Joseph Smith clarified the vague verse in the account in Exodus, saying that it should read: "And he said unto Moses, Thou canst not see my face at this time, lest mine anger be kindled against thee also, and I destroy thee, and thy people; for there shall no man among them see me at this time, and live, for they are exceeding sinful. And no sinful man hath at any time, neither shall there be any sinful man at any time, that shall see my face and live" (JST, Exodus 33:20).

It would appear, then, that what we really need to understand is that if God were to appear to us in His full glory, our mortal bodies would have to undergo a physical change—transfiguration. Otherwise, we would be consumed and burned in His presence. It also appears that in order for us to be transfigured, we must be living an exemplary life. That would also explain how and why the wicked will burn as stubble at the Savior's second coming. President Joseph Fielding Smith said the following concerning the things that Moses experienced and learned:

> Is it not possible that these great orbs that shine in the heavens, many of them thousands of times larger than our sun, are after all celestial globes that have reached their exaltation, rather than the dying worlds of so-called scientific theories? It is the destiny of planets and heavenly bodies to endure forever, for the Almighty has never made anything great or small that was not to be eternal. There is much we do not know, and man is not justified in saying that life cannot exist except under the peculiar conditions, which prevail upon this earth. The scriptures teach us that God lives in everlasting burnings, and the brightness of his coming will be so powerful that when he comes the wicked will be as stubble and will be consumed. Well did Moses say: But now mine own eyes have beheld God; but not my natural, but my spiritual eyes, for my natural eyes

> could not have beheld; for I should have withered and died in his presence; but his glory was upon me; and I beheld his face, for I was transfigured before him. (Moses 1:11.)
>
> Daniel's three companions never could have survived the fire of the furnace heated many times beyond its normal condition if the power of the Almighty had not been upon them. As it was, they came forth without as much as the smell of the flames and smoke upon their clothes. We should not ridicule or doubt the great power of the Lord of hosts. (*Restoration of All Things,* 299)

Thus will it be that when we are resurrected. Everyone who lives worthy to inherit the celestial kingdom of God will be given a body that is able to abide the inherent glory of that eternal world. Apparently, those who fail to qualify for such a degree of glory will receive a body that will be able to abide the degree of glory in which they will reside, but where God and Christ dwell, they cannot come:

> There are some people who have supposed that if we are quickened telestial bodies that eventually, throughout the ages of eternity, we will continue to progress until we will find our place in the celestial kingdom, but the scriptures and revelations of God have said that those who are quickened telestial bodies cannot come where God and Christ dwell, worlds without end. (George Albert Smith, in Conference Report, October 1945, 172)

Rewards or Punishments

With so much valuable information at our disposal about the hereafter, there is no reason for the world to remain in darkness concerning it. From the light we have been given, it is evident that it is up to each of us to choose our own eternal reward. Consider the following quotes:

> The Church does teach that there is a place called hell. Of course we do not believe that all those who do not receive the gospel will eventually be cast into hell. We do not believe that hell is a place where the wicked are being burned forever. The Lord has prepared a place, however, for all those who are to be eternally punished for the violation of his laws. In Section 76 of the Doctrine and Covenants the Lord has given us the clearest and most complete information in revelation to the salvation of mankind and the punishment of the wicked. Briefly stated it is this:
>
> INDIVIDUALS TO BE GRADED: 1. The celestial kingdom is prepared for the righteous, those who have been faithful in the keeping of the commandments of the Lord, and have been cleansed of all their sins. These dwell in the presence of the Father and the Son. They become like the Son and are joint heirs with him in the Father's kingdom. The Bible teaches this, for instance, see Romans 8:12–17, and 1 Corinthians 15.
>
> 2. The terrestrial kingdom. Into this kingdom will go all those who have lived clean lives, but were not willing to receive the gospel; also those who have lived clean lives but who, notwithstanding their membership in the Church, were not valiant, and those who refused to receive the gospel when they lived on the earth, but in the spirit world accepted the testimony of Jesus. All who enter this kingdom must be of that class who have been morally clean.
>
> 3. The telestial kingdom. Into this kingdom will go all of those who have been unclean in their lives. See verses 98 to 112, in Section 76.

> These people who enter there will be the unclean; the liars, sorcerers, adulterers, and those who have broken their covenants. Of these the Lord says: These are they who are cast down to hell and suffer the wrath of Almighty God, until the fulness of times, when Christ shall have subdued all enemies under his feet, and shall have perfected his work. (D&C 76:106.)
>
> Yet these, after they have been punished for their sins and having been turned over to the torments of Satan, shall eventually come forth, after the millennium, to receive the telestial kingdom—
>
> For they shall be judged according to their works, and every man shall receive according to his own works, his own dominion, in the mansions which are prepared. And they shall be servants of the Most High; but where God and Christ dwell they cannot come. (Ibid., 76:111–12.)
>
> 4. A place where those who cannot be redeemed and who are called sons of Perdition will go into outer darkness. This is the real hell where those who once knew the truth and had the testimony of it and then turned away and blasphemed the name of Jesus Christ, will go. These are they who have sinned against the Holy Ghost. (See Matthew 12:31–32.) For them there is no forgiveness, and the Lord said he had prepared a place for them. (D&C 76:31–37; 88:32–33.) (Smith, *Answers to Gospel Questions,* 2:209)

In summary, I quote again from President Joseph Fielding Smith:

> All those who enter the telestial kingdom, which will be a place, as each of these kingdoms will be, will be punished for their sins. Satan for a time will have dominion over them until they

> have paid the price of their sinning, before they can enter into that telestial kingdom.
>
> This earth will become a celestial kingdom when it is sanctified. Those who enter the terrestrial kingdom will have to go to some other sphere which will be prepared for them. Those who enter the telestial kingdom, likewise will have to go to some earth which is prepared for them, and there will be another place which is hell where the devil and those who are punished to go with him will dwell. Of course, those who enter the telestial kingdom, and those who enter the terrestrial kingdom will have the eternal punishment which will come to them in knowing that they might, if they had kept the commandments of the Lord, have returned to his presence as his sons and his daughters. This will be a torment to them, and in that sense it will be hell. (Smith, *Answers to Gospel Questions,* 2:49)

It doesn't really matter if we were born into the covenant or adopted into it. The parable of the laborers would definitely seem to apply to the obtaining of our final reward. It seems clear that neither the sins that we commit nor the works that we do will ultimately determine our eternal reward. It will just matter what we have become.

The words of Elder Dallin H. Oaks illustrate this point:

> The Master's reward in the Final Judgment will not be based on how long we have labored in the vineyard. We do not obtain our heavenly reward by punching a time clock. What is essential is that our labors in the workplace of the Lord have caused us to *become* something. For some of us, this requires a longer time than for others. What is important in the end is what we have become by our labors. Many who come in the eleventh hour have been refined and prepared

by the Lord in ways other than formal employment in the vineyard. These workers are like the prepared dry mix to which it is only necessary to "add water"—the perfecting ordinance of baptism and the gift of the Holy Ghost. With that addition—even in the eleventh hour—these workers are in the same state of development and qualified to receive the same reward as those who have labored long in the vineyard. ("The Challenge to Become," *Ensign,* November 2000, 34)

Chapter 15

Eternal Life

In my Father's house are many mansions: if it were not so, I would have told you. I go to prepare a place for you. And if I go and prepare a place for you, I will come again, and receive you unto myself; that where I am, there ye may be also.

—John 14:2–3

Eternal life is defined as the type of life that our Father in Heaven lives. He and the Only Begotten Son have overcome all things and have achieved a condition of perfection. He has commanded us, His spirit children, to likewise strive for that same condition in our own individual lives: "Be ye therefore perfect, even as your Father which is in heaven is perfect" (Matthew 5:48).

No one will ever achieve that status while in this mortal life, but that does not excuse us from the obligation of trying to reach it. Just as our earthly parents usually desire the best for each of us, so likewise our Heavenly Father desires that we each find joy, happiness, and fulfillment in our quest for eternal life. He will do all within His means to help us toward the goal of becoming as He is. However, if we expect to see our goal through to fruition, we must be willing to strive each day to do as the Savior did.

Though it was a difficult thing for Him to do, Jesus carried through with His Father's plan to provide the Atonement for mankind. Three times, as He paid the price for our sins and our sorrows in the Garden of Gethsemane, he appealed to His Father to provide an alternate way, if it was at all possible. It doesn't appear that he was too excited by the prospect of suffering the pains of hell, all alone (Matthew 26:37–47).

Because Jesus put His entire trust in His Father, we are offered the opportunity to be cleansed from our earthly sins and transgressions. It therefore behooves each of us to appreciate that selfless sacrifice made in our behalf and take advantage of His extended hand. As we repent of our sins and truly become born again, we will become increasingly as He and the Father are—perfect. That is the goal He has set for us, but it all hinges upon our submitting our will, as He did, to that of the Father. In this manner and only in this manner can the full measure of the atonement of Jesus Christ be extended to heal us from our fallen state. Only then can its healing power through the aid of the Holy Ghost make of us a new person, cleansed from all sin and iniquity unto sanctification—a process we chose to participate in during our earthly sojourn and finish in the eternities.

A modern prophet, President Ezra Taft Benson, has said: "Men and women who turn their lives over to God will discover that He can make a lot more out of their lives than they can. He will deepen their joys, expand their vision, quicken their minds, strengthen their muscles, lift their spirits, multiply their blessings, increase their opportunities, comfort their souls, raise up friends, and pour out peace. Whoever will lose his life in the service of God will find eternal life" (*The Teachings of Ezra Taft Benson,* 361).

The scriptures teach us some interesting things about the Savior, but what we don't have is a record of the formative years of His life. When I was growing up, I suppose I just always assumed that He was born with everything He ever acquired. In a sense, I pictured Him as this little Messiah in His crib, just lying there with all of this great knowledge.

The New Testament Gospels deal with the three-year period of Jesus Christ's ministry. We have a couple of chapters devoted to His birth, but by and large what they really cover is His life from age thirty until his crucifixion and resurrection at age thirty-three. So what of His formative years, boyhood, adolescence, and adult life to age thirty? What do we know of those years? Not a lot. The scriptures tell us:

> And the child grew, and waxed strong in spirit, filled with wisdom: and the grace of God was upon him.
>
> Now his parents went to Jerusalem every year at the feast of the passover. And when he was twelve years old, they went up to Jerusalem after the custom of the feast.
>
> And when they had fulfilled the days, as they returned, the child Jesus tarried behind in Jerusalem; and Joseph and his mother knew not of it.
>
> But they, supposing him to have been in the company, went a day's journey; and they sought him among their kinsfolk and acquaintance. And when they found him not, they turned back again to Jerusalem, seeking him.
>
> And it came to pass, that after three days they found him in the temple, sitting in the midst of the doctors, both hearing them, and asking them questions. And all that heard him were astonished at his understanding and answers.
>
> And when they saw him, they were amazed:

> and his mother said unto him, Son, why hast thou thus dealt with us? Behold, thy father and I have sought thee sorrowing.
>
> And he said unto them, How is it that ye sought me? Wist ye not that I must be about my Father's business? And they understood not the saying which he spake unto them.
>
> And he went down with them, and came to Nazareth, and was subject unto them: but his mother kept all these sayings in her heart.
>
> And Jesus increased in wisdom and stature, and in favour with God and man. (Luke 2:40–52)

From this passage we can see that by the time He was twelve years old, Jesus knew who He was. At least it indicates that by then He knew who His "real" father was. The information we have in the final two verses of chapter two seems to offer us the most detail about his young life. He returned home, was subject to Joseph and Mary, and increased in wisdom, stature, and favor with both God and man.

The next we hear of Him is when He goes to the Jordan River to receive His baptism by John. So what of those eighteen years between twelve and thirty? For some insight to that question, let us go to the book of Hebrews:

> For every high priest taken from among men is ordained for men in things pertaining to God, that he may offer both gifts and sacrifices for sins:
>
> Who can have compassion on the ignorant, and on them that are out of the way; for that he himself also is compassed with infirmity. And by reason hereof he ought, as for the people, so also for himself, to offer for sins.
>
> And no man taketh this honour unto himself, but he that is called of God, as was Aaron.
>
> So also Christ glorified not himself to be made an high priest; but he that said unto him,

> Thou art my Son, to day have I begotten thee.
>
> As he saith also in another place, Thou art a priest for ever after the order of Melchisedec.
>
> Who in the days of his flesh, when he had offered up prayers and supplications with strong crying and tears unto him that was able to save him from death, and was heard in that he feared;
>
> Though he were a Son, yet learned he obedience by the things which he suffered; and being made perfect, he became the author of eternal salvation unto all them that obey him;
>
> Called of God an high priest after the order of Melchisedec. (Hebrews 5:1–10)

Some will say that these verses speak of Abraham, but it appears that they have a dual interpretation, as is the case with many other scripture references. Nevertheless, Abraham is not the author of salvation. That distinction belongs to only one, and that one is Jesus Christ: "Moreover, I say unto you, that there shall be no other name given nor any other way nor means whereby salvation can come unto the children of men, only in and through the name of Christ, the Lord Omnipotent" (Mosiah 3:17).

So it appears that Jesus learned from the experiences of life, just as we do. We get some additional insight from modern revelation as well into His pattern of learning:

"Wherefore, the Almighty God gave his Only Begotten Son, as it is written in those scriptures which have been given of him. He suffered temptations but gave no heed unto them" (D&C 20:21–22).

The Savior apparently grew and developed in much the same manner that each of us does. So what is the difference between Him and us? When He learned something, He lived it. Most of us seem to get some inherent thrill out of living life on the edge. I guess it gives us a rush to see how close to the edge of sin and disaster we can possibly get, without falling over the edge. Christ did not live His life in that manner. He lived as He taught we should live:

He admonishes us, "Therefore I would that ye should be perfect even as I, or your Father who is in heaven is perfect" (3 Nephi 12:48).

It would seem that it was in the suffering of temptations and not giving them heed and in the suffering He endured for each of us, both in the garden and on the cross, that Christ was able to really come to know what each of us will go through. That is why only He is qualified to be our judge. I might say to you when you are going through a difficult time, that I understand your pain. The fact is, neither I nor anyone else can truly understand what you're going through because we're not you. But as we have discussed, Christ suffered for all of our sins, and he suffered before we did. Therefore He is qualified to give a true unbiased judgment. Perhaps that is why He has forbidden us to judge our neighbors of their sins and shortcomings.

> My disciples, in days of old, sought occasion against one another and forgave not one another in their hearts; and for this evil they were afflicted and sorely chastened.
>
> Wherefore, I say unto you, that ye ought to forgive one another; for he that forgiveth not his brother his trespasses standeth condemned before the Lord; for there remaineth in him the greater sin. I, the Lord, will forgive whom I will forgive, but of you it is required to forgive all men.
>
> And ye ought to say in your hearts—let God judge between me and thee, and reward thee according to thy deeds. (D&C 64:8–11)

If we had gone through the Garden of Gethsemane for others' sins, maybe we would be fit to make a judgment on the life or behavior of others, but as we know, only He did that.

Having gone through what He did (not just for us but with us), Jesus gained true empathy for each of us and our individual situations. He knows what we are going through and feeling because He vicariously went through every one of those experiences long before we did. The following excerpts from the words of Elder Neal A. Maxwell are somewhat lengthy, but I include them because of the insight they shed on just how far-reaching and personal the Savior's suffering for each of us was:

President Brigham Young spoke of what evoked the "why" from Jesus, saying that during the axis of agony which was Gethsemane and Calvary, the Father at some point withdrew both His presence and His Spirit from Jesus (see *Journal of Discourses* 3:205–6). Thereby Jesus' personal triumph was complete and His empathy perfected. Having "descended below all things," He comprehends, perfectly and personally, the full range of human suffering! (see D&C 88:6; 122:8).

A spiritual sung in yesteryear has an especially moving and insightful line: "Nobody knows the troubles I've seen, nobody knows but Jesus" (see also Alma 7:11–12). Truly, Jesus was exquisitely "acquainted with grief," as no one else (Isaiah 53:3). ("Apply the Atoning Blood of Christ," *Ensign,* November 1997)

Thus, the daily taking up of the cross means daily denying ourselves the appetites of the flesh.

By emulating the Master, who endured temptations but "gave no heed unto them," we, too, can live in a world filled with temptations "such as [are] common to man" (1 Corinthians 10:13) Of course Jesus noticed the tremendous temptations that came to him, but He did not process and reprocess them. Instead, He rejected them promptly. If we entertain temptations, soon they begin entertaining us! Turning these unwanted lodgers away at the doorstep of the mind is one way of giving "no heed." Besides, these would-be lodgers are actually barbarians who, if admitted, can be evicted only with great trauma.

In a decaying environment, the mind is the last redoubt of righteousness, and it must be preserved even amid bombardment by evil stimuli. Christ is competent to see us through, "for in that he himself hath suffered being tempted, He is able to succour them that are tempted" (Hebrews 2:18).

As promised, He will make either "a way to escape" or a way "to bear it" (1 Corinthians 10:13).

We surely have been warned and forewarned about our time, a period in which the compression of challenges may make a year seem like a decade. Members will be cleverly mocked and scorned by those in the "great and spacious building," representing the pride of the world (1 Nephi 8:26; 1 Nephi 11:36). No matter, for ere long, He who was raised on the third day will raze that spacious but third-class hotel!

Ours will be a time of great inversion as well as perversion, as some will call good evil and evil good (see Isaiah 5:20; 2 Nephi 15:20; D&C 64:16; 2 Nephi 2:5). Others, in their ignorance of spiritual truths, will "speak evil of those things which they know not" (Jude 1:10; see 2 Peter 2:12).

Peace has already been taken from the earth (see D&C 1:35). Nation will rise against nation (see Matthew 24:7). It will also be a time of hardening as the love of many waxes cold and iniquity abounds (see D&C 45:27). Secular bewilderment will be epidemic amid the "distress of nations, with perplexity" (Luke 21:25). . . .

We cannot expect to live in such a world without experiencing certain consequences of these conditions. Yet we can always keep our covenants, even if we cannot keep such conditions from coming.

The Lord, who knows all that through which we will pass, will help us to overcome in our "small moment" of time (D&C 122:4). If we are settled, we will "endure it well" (D&C 121:8) and "hold fast" (1 Thessalonians 5:21). Endured righteously, "all these things shall give [us] experience, and shall be for [our] good" (D&C 122:7). "Think it not strange" when disciples are called upon to pass through "the fiery trial," said Peter (1 Peter 4:12). Even so, the Saints of God, as prophesied, will eventually "cry unto the Lord day and night until deliverance comes" (*Prophetic Sayings of Heber C. Kimball,* n.p., n.d., p. 6).

The spiritually settled will finally overcome, and the glorious promise is, "To him that overcometh will I grant to sit with me in my throne, even as I also overcame, and am set down with my Father in his throne" (Revelation 3:21).

Meanwhile, let us remember "what manner of persons [we] ought . . . to be" (2 Peter 3:11; 3 Nephi 27:27). Attributively, we are to become even as Jesus, with His virtues being increasingly replicated in our lives. Even in the midst of our obvious imperfections, a sacred process is to be underway—if slowly, nevertheless resolutely. Whatever one's unfolding agendum, he can be overcoming if he is becoming more like Christ!

Even though scarred by the past, if contrite, Jesus' promise is: "I shall heal them" (3 Nephi 18:32). Such shall become "alive again" (Luke 15:32) "in Christ because of [their] faith" (2 Nephi 25:25). As part of His infinite atonement, Jesus knows "according to the flesh" all that through which we pass (Alma 7:11–12). He has borne the sins, griefs, sorrows, and, declared Jacob, the pains of every man, woman, and child (see 2 Nephi 9:21). Having been perfected in His empathy, Jesus thus knows how to succor us.

We can, therefore, actually do as Peter urged and cast our cares upon the Lord (1 Peter 5:7);

He is familiar with them, including even the feeling of being forsaken (see Mark 14:50; 15:34). Nothing is beyond His redeeming reach or His encircling empathy. Therefore, we should not complain about our own life's not being a rose garden when we remember who wore the crown of thorns!

I turn now to the conclusion of Jesus' mortal Messiahship. Luke reported Jesus' sweating in Gethsemane "as it were great drops of blood falling down to the ground" (Luke 22:44). This fact is fully validated in the "other books" of restoration scripture (1 Nephi 13:39–40): "Which suffering caused myself, even God, the greatest of all, . . . to bleed at every pore, and to suffer both body and spirit—and would that I might not drink the bitter cup, and shrink" (D&C 19:18).

The necessary but awesome shedding of Jesus' blood thus occurred not only in the severe scourging, but earlier in Gethsemane. A recent and thoughtful article by several physicians on the physical death of Jesus Christ indicates that "the severe scourging, with its intense pain and appreciable blood loss, most probably left Jesus in a preshock state." (We all recall, of course, that a dramatically weakened Jesus needed help to carry the cross.) "Therefore, even before the actual crucifixion, Jesus' physical condition was at least serious and possibly critical. . . . Although scourging may have resulted in considerable blood loss, crucifixion per se was a relatively bloodless procedure" (*Journal of the American Medical Association,* 21 March 1986, 1458, 1461)

In addition to the consequences of scourging, how Christ's lifeblood had already flowed in Gethsemane! Remember, he suffered "both body and spirit" (D&C 19:18). Declared King Ben-

> jamin, Christ would suffer "even more than man can suffer, except it be unto death; for behold, blood cometh from every pore, so great shall be his anguish" (Mosiah 3:7).
>
> Having bled at every pore, how red His raiment must have been in Gethsemane, how crimson that cloak!
>
> No wonder, when Christ comes in power and glory, that He will come in reminding red attire (see D&C 133:48), signifying not only the winepress of wrath, but also to bring to our remembrance how He suffered for each of us in Gethsemane and on Calvary!
>
> In recent years, as I have sung hymns about the Atonement, it has been with an especially full heart that I sing lines such as "How great thou art," "I scarce can take it in," "To rescue a soul so rebellious and proud as mine," "I stand all amazed," and "Oh, it is wonderful!" (*Hymns,* 1985, nos. 86, 193).
>
> . . . Let not Jesus' redemption of us stop at the immortalizing dimension of the Atonement, "the loosing of the bands of death" (Alma 11:41). Let us grasp the proffered gift of eternal life! We will end up either choosing Christ's manner of living or His manner of suffering! It is either "suffer even as I" (D&C 19:16–17), or overcome "even as [He] . . . overcame" (Revelation 3:21). His beckoning command is to become "even as I am" (3 Nephi 27:27). The spiritually settled accept that invitation, and "through the atonement of Christ," they *become and overcome!* (see Mosiah 3:18, 19). ("'Overcome . . . Even as I Also Overcame,'" *Ensign,* May 1987, 71–72)

This life has been appointed unto each of us to prepare us for salvation in the eternities. Therefore, to each of us who overcome the trials and tests, hardships, and temptations of this life, we are given a true gift of grace from that very Savior who also overcame all. He has said: "Behold, I stand at the door, and knock: if any man hear my voice, and open the door, I will come in to him, and will sup with him, and he with me. To him that overcometh will I grant to sit with me in my throne, even as I also overcame, and am set down with my Father in his throne" (Revelation 3:20–21).

What is our Savior is promising us if we will, through His help, overcome the trials and temptations of this earth life? The Apostle Paul, whom the Christian world relies upon heavily on for its dogma, sheds some light on this mystery:

> There is therefore now no condemnation to them which are in Christ Jesus, who walk not after the flesh, but after the Spirit. For the law of the Spirit of life in Christ Jesus hath made me free from the law of sin and death.
>
> For what the law could not do, in that it was weak through the flesh, God sending his own Son in the likeness of sinful flesh, and for sin, condemned sin in the flesh:
>
> That the righteousness of the law might be fulfilled in us, who walk not after the flesh, but after the Spirit.
>
> For they that are after the flesh do mind the things of the flesh; but they that are after the Spirit the things of the Spirit. For to be carnally minded is death; but to be spiritually minded is life and peace.
>
> Because the carnal mind is enmity against God: for it is not subject to the law of God, neither indeed can be.
>
> So then they that are in the flesh cannot please God. But ye are not in the flesh, but in the Spirit, if so be that the Spirit of God dwell in you. Now if any man have not the Spirit of Christ, he is none of his.

> And if Christ be in you, the body is dead because of sin; but the Spirit is life because of righteousness.
>
> But if the Spirit of him that raised up Jesus from the dead dwell in you, he that raised up Christ from the dead shall also quicken your mortal bodies by his Spirit that dwelleth in you.
>
> Therefore, brethren, we are debtors, not to the flesh, to live after the flesh.
>
> For if ye live after the flesh, ye shall die: but if ye through the Spirit do mortify the deeds of the body, ye shall live.
>
> For as many as are led by the Spirit of God, they are the sons of God. For ye have not received the spirit of bondage again to fear; but ye have received the Spirit of adoption, whereby we cry, Abba, Father.
>
> The Spirit itself beareth witness with our spirit, that we are the children of God:
>
> And if children, then heirs; heirs of God, and joint-heirs with Christ; if so be that we suffer with him, that we may be also glorified together. (Romans 8:1–17)

I have been a licensed financial services agent for a number of years, and as I've set up life insurance policies for my clients, it has been necessary for them to designate beneficiaries in the event of their untimely demise. A beneficiary is one who inherits the proceeds of what the policy owner leaves to them. Often individuals will designate the funds to go to each of their children jointly. This legally makes each child a "joint-heir" to those benefits.

What, then, is the Apostle Paul speaking of when he told the Saints (members of the Church) at Rome, that each of us who is willing to be partakers of Christ's atonement will be joint-heirs with Him of the Father's blessings and that we'll be glorified together? In light of what it truly means to be a joint-heir, I would submit that what Paul means is precisely what he is saying. We are all sons and daughters of the Living

God, and we who have entered the waters of baptism through the power of the holy priesthood have become adopted sons and daughters of Jesus Christ. As his adopted children, and joint-heirs, we are entitled to all that he is entitled to. And what would that mean? Lest we think that we are misinterpreting the doctrines that Paul was teaching here, let us continue to search his writings, looking for a common thread in his different letters concerning this topic:

> Let this mind be in you, which was also in Christ Jesus: Who, being in the form of God, thought it not robbery to be equal with God:
>
> But made himself of no reputation, and took upon him the form of a servant, and was made in the likeness of men:
>
> And being found in fashion as a man, he humbled himself, and became obedient unto death, even the death of the cross.
>
> Wherefore God also hath highly exalted him, and given him a name which is above every name:
>
> That at the name of Jesus every knee should bow, of things in heaven, and things in earth, and things under the earth;
>
> And that every tongue should confess that Jesus Christ is Lord, to the glory of God the Father.
>
> Wherefore, my beloved, as ye have always obeyed, not as in my presence only, but now much more in my absence, work out your own salvation with fear and trembling.
>
> For it is God which worketh in you both to will and to do of his good pleasure. (Philippians 2:5–13)

We need to examine a few different things in this particular passage if we are going to understand what Paul is teaching. We'll begin with verse 6, which indicates that Christ was equal with God, His Father. Most of the Christian world would not consider this a particular problem because they believe that God the Father and Jesus Christ are different manifestations of the same personage. This assumption, however, is in error. In chapter 17 of the Gospel of John, as the Savior is preparing to go into the Garden of Gethsemane to offer up the Atonement for the ransom of all mankind, he offers what I consider the greatest prayer ever uttered. It is the great Intercessory Prayer, and in it he addresses His Father, thanking Him for giving unto Him those who have chosen to become His adopted sons and daughters.

> These words spake Jesus, and lifted up his eyes to heaven, and said, Father, the hour is come; glorify thy Son, that thy Son also may glorify thee:
>
> As thou hast given him power over all flesh, that he should give eternal life to as many as thou hast given him.
>
> And this is life eternal, that they might know thee the only true God, and Jesus Christ, whom thou hast sent.
>
> I have glorified thee on the earth: I have finished the work which thou gavest me to do.
>
> And now, O Father, glorify thou me with thine own self with the glory which I had with thee before the world was.
>
> I have manifested thy name unto the men which thou gavest me out of the world: thine they were, and thou gavest them me; and they have kept thy word.
>
> Now they have known that all things whatsoever thou hast given me are of thee.
>
> For I have given unto them the words which thou gavest me; and they have received them, and have known surely that I came out from thee, and they have believed that thou didst send me.
>
> I pray for them: I pray not for the world, but for them which thou hast given me; for they are thine.

> And all mine are thine, and thine are mine; and I am glorified in them.
>
> And now I am no more in the world, but these are in the world, and I come to thee. Holy Father, keep through thine own name those whom thou hast given me, that they may be one, as we are. (John 17:1–11)

Many have mistakenly assumed that in saying that He and the Father are one, Jesus is implying that their unity is literal. Similar allusions appear in the Book of Mormon and the Doctrine and Covenants. However, as we continue reading this sacred prayer, the Savior makes the context in which He refers to the word *one* unequivocally clear:

> I have given them thy word; and the world hath hated them, because they are not of the world, even as I am not of the world.
>
> I pray not that thou shouldest take them out of the world, but that thou shouldest keep them from the evil.
>
> They are not of the world, even as I am not of the world. Sanctify them through thy truth: thy word is truth. As thou hast sent me into the world, even so have I also sent them into the world.
>
> And for their sakes I sanctify myself, that they also might be sanctified through the truth.
>
> Neither pray I for these alone, but for them also which shall believe on me through their word;
>
> That they all may be one; as thou, Father, art in me, and I in thee, that they also may be one in us: that the world may believe that thou hast sent me.
>
> And the glory which thou gavest me I have given them; that they may be one, even as we are one: I in them, and thou in me, that they

> may be made perfect in one; and that the world may know that thou hast sent me, and hast loved them, as thou hast loved me.
>
> Father, I will that they also, whom thou hast given me, be with me where I am; that they may behold my glory, which thou hast given me: for thou lovedst me before the foundation of the world. (John 17:14–24)

In just what sense can you and I become one in each other? Can you become me? Can I become you? Or can you or I ever really become anyone other than who we are? If we are sincerely interested in truth, we know the answer! Yet we find Jesus pleading with His Father that we may all "be one" in the same way that He and His Father are one. Why would the Bible record Christ as praying to Himself? That would seem to make as little sense as two people being the same person, would it not? And when He hung on the cross at Golgotha and the pains of Gethsemane returned, what was the purpose of the cry He made in His agony?

> And about the ninth hour Jesus cried with a loud voice, saying, Eli, Eli, lama sabachthani? That is to say, My God, my God, why hast thou forsaken me?
>
> Some of them that stood there, when they heard that, said, This man calleth for Elias. And straightway one of them ran, and took a spunge, and filled it with vinegar, and put it on a reed, and gave him to drink. The rest said, Let be, let us see whether Elias will come to save him. Jesus, when he had cried again with a loud voice, yielded up the ghost. (Matthew 27:46–50)

The Prophet Joseph Smith revealed this important doctrine concerning the Godhead:

> The Father has a body of flesh and bones as tangible as man's; the Son also; but the Holy

> Ghost has not a body of flesh and bones, but is a personage of Spirit. Were it not so, the Holy Ghost could not dwell in us.
>
> A man may receive the Holy Ghost, and it may descend upon him and not tarry with him. (D&C 130:22–23)

In his epistle to the Corinthian Saints and to the Saints at Caesarea Philippi, the Apostle Paul gives us further insight into what "being one" means:

> Now I beseech you, brethren, by the name of our Lord Jesus Christ, that ye all speak the same thing, and that there be no divisions among you; but that ye be perfectly joined together in the same mind and in the same judgment.
>
> For it hath been declared unto me of you, my brethren, by them which are of the house of Chloe, that there are contentions among you.
>
> Now this I say, that every one of you saith, I am of Paul; and I of Apollos; and I of Cephas; and I of Christ.
>
> Is Christ divided? Was Paul crucified for you? or were ye baptized in the name of Paul?
>
> I thank God that I baptized none of you, but Crispus and Gaius;
>
> Lest any should say that I had baptized in mine own name. (1 Corinthians 1:10–15)

> If there be therefore any consolation in Christ, if any comfort of love, if any fellowship of the Spirit, if any bowels and mercies,
>
> Fulfil ye my joy, that ye be likeminded, having the same love, being of one accord, of one mind.
>
> Let nothing be done through strife or vainglory; but in lowliness of mind let each esteem other better than themselves.

> Look not every man on his own things, but every man also on the things of others.
>
> Let this mind be in you, which was also in Christ Jesus: Who, being in the form of God, thought it not robbery to be equal with God. (Philippians 2:1–6)

Just as members of an athletic team must play as one if they want to be successful, so we must be of one heart and one mind, as Jesus Christ and His Father are. By submitting His will to that of His Father, the Savior showed His oneness with His Father, and it now behooves each of us to strive to do likewise. According to the teachings of Paul, if we do so, we will inherit the glory that the Father and the Son enjoy. Remember what the scripture in John said: "And the glory which thou gavest me I have given them; that they may be one, even as we are one" (John 17:22).

Thus we have learned the following: (1) Christ and His Father are separate and distinct individuals of flesh and bones. (2) Christ and His Father are one in purpose because the Son did everything His Father would do in all situations. They are of the same heart and mind. (3) Those who join Christ's Church through baptism become His adopted sons and daughters. (4) Christ was made equal with God the Father. (5) As we become like Christ, He will give us of the same glory that His Father gave unto Him. As His adopted sons and daughters, we become joint-heirs with Christ of all that He inherits.

Therefore, it would appear that all who choose to follow the Savior with full purpose of heart, entering into sacred covenants that are performed by authorized servants who hold the holy priesthood, and then strive to keep those covenants until the end of their mortal lives, will enter into the rest of the Lord in the next life. They will be partakers of all that the Father and the Son have. That type of eternal reward is referred to in the scriptures as eternal life.

Now, if Christ is equal with God the Eternal Father, being His heir would make him an inheritor of godhood. So what would that mean to those of us who become Christ's adopted sons and daughters, thus becoming joint-heirs with Christ? Paul says:

> Not as though I had already attained, either were already perfect: but I follow after, if that I may apprehend that for which also I am apprehended of Christ Jesus.
>
> Brethren, I count not myself to have apprehended: but this one thing I do, forgetting those things which are behind, and reaching forth unto those things which are before,
>
> I press toward the mark for the prize of the high calling of God in Christ Jesus.
>
> Let us therefore, as many as be perfect, be thus minded: and if in any thing ye be otherwise minded, God shall reveal even this unto you.
>
> Nevertheless, whereto we have already attained, let us walk by the same rule, let us mind the same thing.
>
> Brethren, be followers together of me, and mark them which walk so as ye have us for an ensample.
>
> (For many walk, of whom I have told you often, and now tell you even weeping, that they are the enemies of the cross of Christ:
>
> Whose end is destruction, whose God is their belly, and whose glory is in their shame, who mind earthly things.)
>
> For our conversation is in heaven; from whence also we look for the Saviour, the Lord Jesus Christ:
>
> Who shall change our vile body, that it may be fashioned like unto his glorious body, according to the working whereby he is able even to subdue all things unto himself. (Philippians 3:12–21)

Paul was already an apostle of Jesus Christ. What higher calling could he attain? What calling was he pressing toward? One that would require him to strive toward perfection in order to obtain it. He said he was pressing toward the high calling of *God.* Those are Paul's exact words, and either he spoke the truth or he was a liar. If he spoke the truth, then becoming as Christ and His Father are is attainable for us as their heirs, though we will have eternities to work toward that condition. If he was a liar, then we must throw out his doctrinal teachings, which doctrines are virtually all of the doctrines of modern-day Christianity! The gospel is not a smorgasbord, where we can take the things that look good to us and conveniently ignore the rest. Many in the Christian world have looked at The Church of Jesus Christ of Latter-day Saints as being blasphemous for adhering to this particular doctrine, but it appears that we are not the first to teach it and strive toward it. The Apostle Paul also taught it to the ancient Church as well. The Lord revealed this doctrine to the Prophet Joseph Smith:

> Therefore, if a man marry him a wife in the world, and he marry her not by me nor by my word, and he covenant with her so long as he is in the world and she with him, their covenant and marriage are not of force when they are dead, and when they are out of the world; therefore, they are not bound by any law when they are out of the world.
>
> Therefore, when they are out of the world they neither marry nor are given in marriage; but are appointed angels in heaven, which angels are ministering servants, to minister for those who are worthy of a far more, and an exceeding, and an eternal weight of glory.
>
> For these angels did not abide my law; therefore, they cannot be enlarged, but remain separately and singly, without exaltation, in their saved condition, to all eternity; and from henceforth are not gods, but are angels of God forever and ever.
>
> And again, verily I say unto you, if a man marry a wife, and make a covenant with her for time and for all eternity, if that covenant is not by me or by my word, which is my law, and is

not sealed by the Holy Spirit of promise, through him whom I have anointed and appointed unto this power, then it is not valid neither of force when they are out of the world, because they are not joined by me, saith the Lord, neither by my word; when they are out of the world it cannot be received there, because the angels and the gods are appointed there, by whom they cannot pass; they cannot, therefore, inherit my glory; for my house is a house of order, saith the Lord God.

And again, verily I say unto you, if a man marry a wife by my word, which is my law, and by the new and everlasting covenant, and it is sealed unto them by the Holy Spirit of promise, by him who is anointed, unto whom I have appointed this power and the keys of this priesthood; and it shall be said unto them—Ye shall come forth in the first resurrection; and if it be after the first resurrection, in the next resurrection; and shall inherit thrones, kingdoms, principalities, and powers, dominions, all heights and depths—then shall it be written in the Lamb's Book of Life, that he shall commit no murder whereby to shed innocent blood, and if ye abide in my covenant, and commit no murder whereby to shed innocent blood, it shall be done unto them in all things whatsoever my servant hath put upon them, in time, and through all eternity; and shall be of full force when they are out of the world; and they shall pass by the angels, and the gods, which are set there, to their exaltation and glory in all things, as hath been sealed upon their heads, which glory shall be a fulness and a continuation of the seeds forever and ever.

Then shall they be gods, because they have no end; therefore shall they be from everlasting to everlasting, because they continue; then shall

> they be above all, because all things are subject unto them. Then shall they be gods, because they have all power, and the angels are subject unto them. (D&C 132:15–20)

Let's make note what is being said about the condition of the Savior and of all those who overcome the world as He did. In Hebrews we read:

> God, who at sundry times and in divers manners spake in time past unto the fathers by the prophets, hath in these last days spoken unto us by his Son, whom he hath appointed heir of all things, by whom also he made the worlds;
>
> Who being the brightness of his glory, and the express image of his person, and upholding all things by the word of his power, when he had by himself purged our sins, sat down on the right hand of the Majesty on high;
>
> Being made so much better than the angels, as he hath by inheritance obtained a more excellent name than they.
>
> For unto which of the angels said he at any time, Thou art my Son, this day have I begotten thee? And again, I will be to him a Father, and he shall be to me a Son?
>
> And again, when he bringeth in the firstbegotten into the world, he saith, And let all the angels of God worship him. . . .
>
> But to which of the angels said he at any time, Sit on my right hand, until I make thine enemies thy footstool?
>
> Are they not all ministering spirits, sent forth to minister for them who shall be heirs of salvation? (Hebrews 1:1–6, 13–14)

Who is above an angel? Only someone like God. Great are the blessings promised to all of those who overcome the world as the Savior did:

> For we are made partakers of Christ, if we hold the beginning of our confidence stedfast unto the end. (Hebrews 3:14)

> He that hath an ear, let him hear what the Spirit saith unto the churches; to him that overcometh will I give to eat of the tree of life, which is in the midst of the paradise of God. (Revelation 2:7)

> And he that overcometh, and keepeth my works unto the end, to him will I give power over the nations:
>
> And he shall rule them with a rod of iron; as the vessels of a potter shall they be broken to shivers: even as I received of my Father. And I will give him the morning star.
>
> He that hath an ear, let him hear what the Spirit saith unto the churches. (Revelation 2:26–29)

> He that overcometh, the same shall be clothed in white raiment; and I will not blot out his name out of the book of life, but I will confess his name before my Father, and before his angels.
>
> He that hath an ear, let him hear what the Spirit saith unto the churches. (Revelation 3:5–6)

The blessings of exaltation are apparently not just intended for a select few, as some believe. The apostle John, after speaking of twelve thousand special missionaries who are to be called from each of the twelve tribes (for a total of 144,000), says:

> After this I beheld, and, lo, a great multitude, which no man could number, of all nations, and

> kindreds, and people, and tongues, stood before the throne, and before the Lamb, clothed with white robes, and palms in their hands;
>
> And cried with a loud voice, saying, Salvation to our God which sitteth upon the throne, and unto the Lamb.
>
> And all the angels stood round about the throne, and about the elders and the four beasts, and fell before the throne on their faces, and worshipped God,
>
> Saying, Amen: Blessing, and glory, and wisdom, and thanksgiving, and honour, and power, and might, be unto our God for ever and ever. Amen.
>
> And one of the elders answered, saying unto me, What are these which are arrayed in white robes? and whence came they?
>
> And I said unto him, Sir, thou knowest. And he said to me, These are they which came out of great tribulation, and have washed their robes, and made them white in the blood of the Lamb.
>
> Therefore are they before the throne of God, and serve him day and night in his temple: and he that sitteth on the throne shall dwell among them.
>
> They shall hunger no more, neither thirst any more; neither shall the sun light on them, nor any heat.
>
> For the Lamb which is in the midst of the throne shall feed them, and shall lead them unto living fountains of waters: and God shall wipe away all tears from their eyes. (Revelation 7:9–17)

The total number of our Father in Heaven's spirit children who will untimately inherit exaltation may seem small in comparison to all who will be born on the earch. Nevertheless, it is obvious from John's writings that there will still be an innumerable multitude who will overcome the world and, through the grace of the Savior's atonement, enter into the glory of the celestial kingdom. It should come as no surprise that we can become like our Father when we consider the doctrine of sanctification as contained in chapter six. As we attain the state of perfection implied by the term sanctification, we become like the Father and the Son. That is only made possible as we learn to obey eternal law:

> Verily, verily, I say unto you, except ye abide my law ye cannot attain to this glory.
>
> For strait is the gate, and narrow the way that leadeth unto the exaltation and continuation of the lives, and few there be that find it, because ye receive me not in the world neither do ye know me.
>
> But if ye receive me in the world, then shall ye know me, and shall receive your exaltation; that where I am ye shall be also.
>
> This is eternal lives—to know the only wise and true God, and Jesus Christ, whom he hath sent. I am he. Receive ye, therefore, my law. (D&C 132:21–24)

This may seem like a hard doctrine for many to accept, but it is nevertheless a true one. It is quite a simple concept. Everywhere in the day-to-day life of the various living creations of God, we see this same process played out. The offspring will become as the parents are, not as something else. One of the least confusing characteristics of deity is that all things are done in order and according to natural laws of the universe. Therefore, in that same vein, why should it seem a blasphemous doctrine to teach that we can become as our heavenly parents? Indeed, that would seem like a plausible and normal path of progression.

Elder Milton R. Hunter stated:

> "As early as February 16, 1832, the Lord revealed to the Prophet Joseph Smith the sublime truth that "*men may become gods.*" Among many other important truths revealed to Joseph

and Sidney Rigdon that day, God showed them a vision of the three degrees of glory and explained to them who should be assigned to each degree. In speaking of those who should inhabit the celestial world, the Lord said:

They are they who are the church of the first-born. They are they into whose hands the Father has given all things—they are they who are Priests and Kings who have received of his fullness, and of his glory; and are Priests of the Most High, after the order of Melchizedek, which was after the order of Enoch, which was after the order of the Only Begotten Son; Wherefore, as it is written *they are Gods,* even the sons of God. . . . These shall dwell in the presence of God and his Christ for ever and ever.

In June, 1840, Lorenzo Snow formulated the following famous couplet: "*As man is, God once was; as God is, man may become.*" This doctrine, when first announced by the Prophet and later restated by Elder Snow, was astounding to Christendom, since the teachers as well as the laity had long ago ceased to regard man as a being of such magnitude. Even today it is still a doctrine understood primarily by members of The Church of Jesus Christ of Latter-day Saints.

Following the earlier pronouncements of this doctrine, much more light came to earth through the prophets of the last dispensation. For example, in a revelation given to Joseph Smith on May 6, 1833, he learned of Jesus' development in the spirit world and of the unfoldment of His personality in mortality and glorification in post-mortal life wherein "He received a fullness of the glory of the Father." Then the following promise was made to mortals:

For if you keep my commandments you shall

receive of his [God's] fullness, and be glorified in me as I am in the Father; therefore, I say unto you, you shall receive grace for grace.

The glory that Christ received was that of Godhood; therefore, for men to receive the same glory they also shall become Gods. In fact, when the Church leaders during the early period of Mormondom searched the scriptures more carefully, it became very clear to them that the ultimate goal of eternal progression is to receive eternal life, i.e., to become as God is. For this cause the Gospel of Jesus Christ was instituted before the foundation of the world and revealed to mankind from age to age by a gracious Heavenly Father. Of course, it is generally understood that a vast majority of the children of our Heavenly Parents will not obey the Gospel principles and ordinances to the degree requisite to finally exalt themselves unto Godhood, but the possibility is that there are many individuals who will attain that desired goal. For example, Abraham, Isaac and Jacob "have entered into their exaltation according to the promises, and sit upon thrones, and are not angels but are Gods."

President Joseph F. Smith beautifully expressed the foregoing doctrine as follows:

Man is the child of God, formed in the divine image and endowed with divine attributes; and even as the infant son of our earthly father and mother is capable in due time of becoming a man, so the undeveloped offspring of celestial parentage is capable by experience through ages of aeons of evolving into a God.

In the words of Dr. John A. Widtsoe, "God and man are of the same race, differing only in their degrees of advancement." Some additional light is thrown on the subject by Charles W. Pen-

> rose; "To know God we must know ourselves. All the personal attributes which are ascribed to God by inspired men, we find in ourselves. . . . Mormonism does not tend to debase God to the level of man, but to exalt man to the perfection of God." (*Gospel through the Ages,* 105)

The following quote from the *Encyclopedia of Mormonism* gives us further insight into life beyond mortality:

> The postmortal spirit world is an actual place where spirits reside and "where they converse together the same as we do on the earth" (*TPJS,* p. 353). "Life and work and activity all continue in the spirit world. Men have the same talents and intelligence there which they had in this life. They possess the same attitudes, inclinations, and feelings there which they had in this life" (*MD,* p. 762).
>
> The postmortal spirit world is a place of continued preparation and learning. In this sense, it is an extension of mortality. Those who have died without an opportunity to hear the gospel of Jesus Christ will have opportunity to hear and accept it in the spirit world. "The great work in the world of spirits is the preaching of the gospel to those who are imprisoned by sin and false traditions" (*MD,* 762). The faithful elders and sisters who depart this life "continue their labors in the preaching of the gospel of repentance and redemption . . . among those who are in darkness" (D&C 138:57; Smith, 461; *see also* Salvation of the Dead). (*Encyclopedia of Mormonism,* 1408)

Many today struggle in body and spirit because they lack fundamental knowledge concerning what awaits us after physical death. A true knowledge and understanding of the hereafter can provide incredible comfort at the death of loved ones. Perhaps nowhere has this information been revealed more fully than in the Doctrine and Covenants.

The Lord revealed through the Prophet Joseph Smith:

> The heavens were opened upon us, and I beheld the celestial kingdom of God, and the glory thereof, whether in the body or out I cannot tell.
>
> I saw the transcendent beauty of the gate through which the heirs of that kingdom will enter, which was like unto circling flames of fire;
>
> Also the blazing throne of God, whereon was seated the Father and the Son.
>
> I saw the beautiful streets of that kingdom, which had the appearance of being paved with gold.
>
> I saw Father Adam and Abraham; and my father and my mother; my brother Alvin, that has long since slept;
>
> And marveled how it was that he had obtained an inheritance in that kingdom, seeing that he had departed this life before the Lord had set his hand to gather Israel the second time, and had not been baptized for the remission of sins.
>
> Thus came the voice of the Lord unto me, saying: All who have died without a knowledge of this gospel, who would have received it if they had been permitted to tarry, shall be heirs of the celestial kingdom of God;
>
> Also all that shall die henceforth without a knowledge of it, who would have received it with all their hearts, shall be heirs of that kingdom;
>
> For I, the Lord, will judge all men according to their works, according to the desire of their hearts.
>
> And I also beheld that all children who die before they arrive at the years of accountability

> are saved in the celestial kingdom of heaven. (D&C 137:1–10)

A vision received by President Joseph F. Smith adds tremendous additional insight to revelation given through Joseph Smith:

> On the third of October, in the year nineteen hundred and eighteen, I sat in my room pondering over the scriptures;
>
> And reflecting upon the great atoning sacrifice that was made by the Son of God, for the redemption of the world;
>
> And the great and wonderful love made manifest by the Father and the Son in the coming of the Redeemer into the world;
>
> That through his atonement, and by obedience to the principles of the gospel, mankind might be saved.
>
> While I was thus engaged, my mind reverted to the writings of the apostle Peter, to the primitive saints scattered abroad throughout Pontus, Galatia, Cappadocia, and other parts of Asia, where the gospel had been preached after the crucifixion of the Lord.
>
> I opened the Bible and read the third and fourth chapters of the first epistle of Peter, and as I read I was greatly impressed, more than I had ever been before, with the following passages:
>
> "For Christ also hath once suffered for sins, the just for the unjust, that he might bring us to God, being put to death in the flesh, but quickened by the Spirit:
>
> "By which also he went and preached unto the spirits in prison;
>
> "Which sometime were disobedient, when once the long-suffering of God waited in the days of Noah, while the ark was a preparing, wherein

few, that is, eight souls were saved by water." (1 Peter 3:18–20.)

"For for this cause was the gospel preached also to them that are dead, that they might be judged according to men in the flesh, but live according to God in the spirit." (1 Peter 4:6.)

As I pondered over these things which are written, the eyes of my understanding were opened, and the Spirit of the Lord rested upon me, and I saw the hosts of the dead, both small and great.

And there were gathered together in one place an innumerable company of the spirits of the just, who had been faithful in the testimony of Jesus while they lived in mortality;

And who had offered sacrifice in the similitude of the great sacrifice of the Son of God, and had suffered tribulation in their Redeemer's name.

All these had departed the mortal life, firm in the hope of a glorious resurrection, through the grace of God the Father and his Only Begotten Son, Jesus Christ.

I beheld that they were filled with joy and gladness, and were rejoicing together because the day of their deliverance was at hand.

They were assembled awaiting the advent of the Son of God into the spirit world, to declare their redemption from the bands of death.

Their sleeping dust was to be restored unto its perfect frame, bone to his bone, and the sinews and the flesh upon them, the spirit and the body to be united never again to be divided, that they might receive a fulness of joy.

While this vast multitude waited and conversed, rejoicing in the hour of their deliverance from the chains of death, the Son of God appeared, declaring liberty to the captives who had been faithful;

And there he preached to them the everlasting gospel, the doctrine of the resurrection and the redemption of mankind from the fall, and from individual sins on conditions of repentance.

But unto the wicked he did not go, and among the ungodly and the unrepentant who had defiled themselves while in the flesh, his voice was not raised;

Neither did the rebellious who rejected the testimonies and the warnings of the ancient prophets behold his presence, nor look upon his face.

Where these were, darkness reigned, but among the righteous there was peace;

And the saints rejoiced in their redemption, and bowed the knee and acknowledged the Son of God as their Redeemer and Deliverer from death and the chains of hell.

Their countenances shone, and the radiance from the presence of the Lord rested upon them, and they sang praises unto his holy name.

I marveled, for I understood that the Savior spent about three years in his ministry among the Jews and those of the house of Israel, endeavoring to teach them the everlasting gospel and call them unto repentance.

And yet, notwithstanding his mighty works, and miracles, and proclamation of the truth, in great power and authority, there were but few who hearkened to his voice, and rejoiced in his presence, and received salvation at his hands.

But his ministry among those who were dead was limited to the brief time intervening between the crucifixion and his resurrection;

And I wondered at the words of Peter—

wherein he said that the Son of God preached unto the spirits in prison, who sometime were disobedient, when once the long-suffering of God waited in the days of Noah—and how it was possible for him to preach to those spirits and perform the necessary labor among them in so short a time.

And as I wondered, my eyes were opened, and my understanding quickened, and I perceived that the Lord went not in person among the wicked and the disobedient who had rejected the truth, to teach them;

But behold, from among the righteous, he organized his forces and appointed messengers, clothed with power and authority, and commissioned them to go forth and carry the light of the gospel to them that were in darkness, even to all the spirits of men; and thus was the gospel preached to the dead.

And the chosen messengers went forth to declare the acceptable day of the Lord and proclaim liberty to the captives who were bound, even unto all who would repent of their sins and receive the gospel.

Thus was the gospel preached to those who had died in their sins, without a knowledge of the truth, or in transgression, having rejected the prophets.

These were taught faith in God, repentance from sin, vicarious baptism for the remission of sins, the gift of the Holy Ghost by the laying on of hands,

And all other principles of the gospel that were necessary for them to know in order to qualify themselves that they might be judged according to men in the flesh, but live according to God in the spirit.

And so it was made known among the dead, both small and great, the unrighteous as well as the faithful, that redemption had been wrought through the sacrifice of the Son of God upon the cross.

Thus was it made known that our Redeemer spent his time during his sojourn in the world of spirits, instructing and preparing the faithful spirits of the prophets who had testified of him in the flesh;

That they might carry the message of redemption unto all the dead, unto whom he could not go personally, because of their rebellion and transgression, that they through the ministration of his servants might also hear his words. . . .

The Prophet Elijah was to plant in the hearts of the children the promises made to their fathers,

Foreshadowing the great work to be done in the temples of the Lord in the dispensation of the fulness of times, for the redemption of the dead, and the sealing of the children to their parents, lest the whole earth be smitten with a curse and utterly wasted at his coming.

All these and many more, even the prophets who dwelt among the Nephites and testified of the coming of the Son of God, mingled in the vast assembly and waited for their deliverance,

For the dead had looked upon the long absence of their spirits from their bodies as a bondage.

These the Lord taught, and gave them power to come forth, after his resurrection from the dead, to enter into his Father's kingdom, there to be crowned with immortality and eternal life,

And continue thenceforth their labor as had been promised by the Lord, and be partakers of all blessings which were held in reserve for them that love him.

The Prophet Joseph Smith, and my father, Hyrum Smith, Brigham Young, John Taylor, Wilford Woodruff, and other choice spirits who were reserved to come forth in the fulness of times to take part in laying the foundations of the great latter-day work,

Including the building of the temples and the performance of ordinances therein for the redemption of the dead, were also in the spirit world.

I observed that they were also among the noble and great ones who were chosen in the beginning to be rulers in the Church of God.

Even before they were born, they, with many others, received their first lessons in the world of spirits and were prepared to come forth in the due time of the Lord to labor in his vineyard for the salvation of the souls of men.

I beheld that the faithful elders of this dispensation, when they depart from mortal life, continue their labors in the preaching of the gospel of repentance and redemption, through the sacrifice of the Only Begotten Son of God, among those who are in darkness and under the bondage of sin in the great world of the spirits of the dead.

The dead who repent will be redeemed, through obedience to the ordinances of the house of God,

And after they have paid the penalty of their transgressions, and are washed clean, shall receive a reward according to their works, for they are heirs of salvation.

Thus was the vision of the redemption of the dead revealed to me, and I bear record, and

> I know that this record is true, through the blessing of our Lord and Savior, Jesus Christ, even so. Amen. (D&C 138:1–37, 47–60)

In light of this extensive amount of information, there is no valid reason that anyone should go through this mortal life in relative darkness concerning the afterlife. Our Heavenly Father has a systematic plan in place for all of us designed to allow each the opportunity to return someday to dwell with Him in His presence. As we have discovered, its requirements are plain and simple once we understand the whole grand picture. We are the offspring of an immortal and exalted Father. We were created in His image and likeness (Genesis 1:26–27) and, as such, have within us the ability to become as He is. We know that our Father's true desire for us is to have what He has and to become as He is.

We are His creations, His children, and just as any earthly father would want his children to accomplish what he has accomplished, so likewise does our Heavenly Father desire that we have all that He has. It should be noted, however, that everything we accomplish adds glory to Him. In that sense we will never be equal with Him, though we can become like Him and share in His glory. This is the true meaning of exaltation. We are saved by the grace of Christ our Savior, but exaltation comes through His grace according to our obedience to His commandments and in the obtaining and living of His saving ordinances and covenants.

Through His boundless love, He has invited us all to become partakers of the new and everlasting covenant, which is the Gospel of Jesus Christ. As we do so, we help fulfill our Father's eternal plan designed in that grand premortal council and bring to pass His eternal destiny for each of His children: "For behold, this is my work and my glory—to bring to pass the immortality and eternal life of man" (Moses 1:39).

President Gordon B. Hinckley summarized the purpose and blessing of belonging to Christ's modern Church: "This is what the gospel is all about—to make bad men good, and good men better. There is a process of change, a procedure in the Church by which even those who have sinned seriously may come back" *(Be Thou an Example,* 11).

The genius of the restored gospel is clear. It will, if followed and if the Holy Spirit is allowed to lend its help, reform even the vilest of sinners into repentant covenant children of our Heavenly Father and help them become as He is. Once individuals have done all they can to perpetuate the process by accepting and keeping gospel covenants and ordinances, the Savior can step forward and, through the atoning sacrifice that he so graciously and unselfishly wrought in our behalf, complete the cleansing process. This having been done, the new person in Christ can be covered under the law of justification and strive toward sanctification. Then and only then can we be allowed back into God's presence, to dwell with Him and His Son forever, to share in the light of their never-ending glory, to obtain our rest, and, with them, to obtain eternal lives.

Epilogue

For behold, this is my work and my glory—to bring to pass the immortality and eternal life of man.

—Moses 1:39

Contrary to the belief of some, mankind didn't just merely flair into existence. Nor did we evolve with apes from a common ancestor. Our forefathers were not mitochondria or salamanders. No! We are all begotten sons and daughters of heavenly parentage, born in our parents' image and likeness. We don't just live our lives and, upon our death, go to heaven to play harps. This life is part of a well-thought-out plan that has been in operation for eons of time on earth and on other planets like our earth and implemented to help the Father's spirit children grow, experience, and work to become as He is and live the kind of life He lives.

Through His love for us, the Father sent Jesus Christ, His Only Begotten Son in the flesh, to earth to atone for our mistakes and to lend us aid—grace—in returning to His presence. He set the example for us by obtaining the ordinances of salvation for Himself and by sacrificing His will for that of the Father. He also exemplified the eternal principle that service to others helps us to become as the Father is. Everything He does is for his children. His work and His glory is in helping His children to become as He is and inherit what He has. The earth was created as the proving ground, and mortal life was the vehicle to accomplish this goal. Agency was given to each of us to choose for ourselves whether we wanted to adhere to our Father's plan and progress toward eternal life, or go our own direction, thus forfeiting that inheritance.

To help us learn to put Him first in our lives, He implemented the principle of sacrifice. Adam was instructed to offer sacrifice upon an altar, and his posterity was to continue that ritual until the Savior came to offer himself as the ultimate sacrifice to atone for our sins and offer comfort in our times of need. After the Savior's advent, the ritual of sacrifice was done away with, but the principle of sacrifice was perpetuated. We are all now to offer our whole souls as a living sacrifice. We are to put our individual wants and desires on the sacrificial altars of our everyday lives. Joseph Smith taught:

> Let us here observe, that a religion that does not require the sacrifice of all things never has power sufficient to produce the faith necessary unto life and salvation. . . . It was through this sacrifice, and this only, that God has ordained

> that men should enjoy eternal life. . . . When a man has offered in sacrifice all that he has for the truth's sake, not even withholding his life, and believing before God that he has been called to make this sacrifice because he seeks to do His will, he does know, most assuredly, that God does and will accept his sacrifice and offering, and that he has not, nor will not seek His face in vain. Under these circumstances, then, he can obtain the faith necessary for him to lay hold on eternal life." (*Teachings of the Prophet Joseph Smith,* 275–76)

Brother Joseph knew well of what he spoke, following the example of the Savior in sacrificing his own life for the gospel cause, giving up his will to submit to the will of the Father.

Indeed, our main challenge appears to be in overcoming our will and learning to submit to our Father's will, as the Savior was able to do: "So it is that real, personal sacrifice never was placing an animal on the altar. Instead, it is a willingness to put the animal in us upon the altar and letting it be consumed! Such is the sacrifice unto the Lord . . . of a broken heart and a contrite spirit, . . . for the denial of self precedes the full acceptance of Him" (Neal A. Maxwell, "'Deny Yourselves of All Ungodliness,'" *Ensign,* May 1995, 68).

In addition to providing agency, the plan of our Father in Heaven provides prophets, men who commune with His Son and then relate His word to us. These inspired men guide us through the spiritual perils and challenges of mortality. They are the Lord's mouthpiece to his children in mortality. Revelation given through the prophets to the Church is the rock upon which the Savior builds and leads His church (Matthew 16:13–18; Acts 1:2). Counsel and commandments from the prophets is essential if we are to be successful in our earthly venture. These prophets hold the priesthood of God (the power of God, given to man to act in His name), and they use it to bless the lives of the people they are called to serve.

That priesthood is extended to worthy men when they join the Savior's church. They can share in God's power as they administer to

His children. By this power, many miracles are performed, and faith is strengthened. However, perhaps the most important facet of the priesthood is the performing of ordinances. Through the ordinances of the priesthood, God's children can gain complete access to the blessings of the Atonement. Baptism and other ordinances performed by the higher priesthood must be entered into through covenant making. Great spiritual blessings are attached to them if they are kept.

Our Father in Heaven gave us a major aid to help us attain the goal of becoming perfected. That aid is the Sabbath day. It is so easy today to become involved in the thick of thin things that we neglect to nurture the spiritual part of our lives. We find ourselves letting the things that matter most take a backseat to things that are pressing but which matter less. Our Father in Heaven foreknew the conditions and challenges we would face in mortality, and He gave us a special day to rest from our worldly pursuits and labors so we could devote our hearts to Him and His things. Our proper use of this special day plays a critical part in our ability to stay clean and unspotted from the evils and sins of the world. Elder Mark E. Petersen gave a powerful statement regarding Sabbath day observance:

> We can readily see that the observance of the Sabbath is an indication of the depth of our conversion. Our observance or nonobservance of the Sabbath is an unerring measure of our attitude toward the Lord personally and toward His suffering in Gethsemane, His death on the cross, and His resurrection from the dead. It is a sign of whether we are Christians in very deed, or whether our conversion is so shallow that commemoration of His atoning sacrifice means little or nothing to us. ("The Sabbath Day," *Ensign,* May 1975, 49)

At the conclusion of our mortal lives, we will be required to give an accounting of our lives to the Savior, who paid the price for our sins. If we have repented of those sins and thus allowed the atonement of Jesus Christ to make us clean, and if we have received all of the saving ordinances of the gospel by the proper authority and become Christ's adopted children, then we will be allowed to inherit along with Him all that the Father has. We will then be able to enjoy throughout the eternities the type of life the Father and the Son enjoy. Through the process of sanctification, we will become as they are, for we will have passed the test of mortality and overcome the things of the world, just as they have. Then and only then will our Father's work and glory concerning this earth be complete. We will have added to His glory and His stature, for He has declared: "For behold, this is my work and my glory—to bring to pass the immortality and eternal life of man" (Moses 1:39).

Scriptural Resources

The Plan

Pre-earth

D&C 29:31–32—Spiritual creation of all things.

Isaiah 14:9–19; D&C 76:25–29—Satan's pre-mortal rebellion and expulsion.

Revelation 12:1–9—The third part of Heavenly Father's spirit children followed Satan and were thrust out with him.

D&C 93:39—Satan's goal is to destroy the souls of man.

Genesis 1—Physical creation.

John 1:1–3, 10, 14—Jesus Christ created the earth.

Genesis 2:1–3; Doctrine & Covenants 59:9–13—The Sabbath day established.

The Fall of Man

James 4:17—Definition of sin (knowing truth and then choosing not to follow it)

Hebrews 10:26—Sin is willfully going against the things of God.

1 Timothy 2:14—Adam was not deceived by Satan, but Eve was.

Genesis 1:26–27; Moses 2:26–28—Adam and Eve were created in the express image of their Father and were given dominion over the earth and all thereon.

Genesis 2:16–17—Adam, not Eve, was given the command by God not to partake of the fruit.

Genesis 1:28—They are commanded to multiply and replenish (fill) the earth.

Moses 3:15–17—Adam is given agency to eat of the tree and he was given the consequence of mortality and physical death if he chose to do so.

Moses 4:5–19; Genesis 3:1–7—Satan tempted Adam through Eve. Adam partook to remain with his wife, as God had commanded him.

Genesis 3:22; Moses 4:27–28—It wasn't until after Adam and Eve partook that their eyes were opened.

Moses 5:2—Adam and Eve become mortal and have adequate knowledge to bear children.

Genesis 4:1—Adam and Eve can now fulfill God's first command to have children.

Moses 5:10–12—Adam and Eve rejoiced over their decision to leave the garden.

2 Nephi 2:15–24—The necessity of the fall of Man is made known.

2 Nephi 2:25—Adam's fall becomes mankind's blessing, not their curse.

D&C 29:33–44; Articles of Faith 1:2—The purpose and benefit of the Fall are summarized.

Redemption (The Role of Jesus Christ)

1 Peter 1:18–20; Revelation 13:8—Christ was foreordained as our Savior.

John 1:1–3—Jesus Christ created this earth.

Exodus 3:1–6, 14; 6:1–3; Isaiah 41:4; 43:11; 45:21; Acts 4:10–12—Jesus Christ is Jehovah, the God of the Old Testament. He gave Israel the Ten Commandments and the Law of Moses, and beside Him there is no Savior.

Romans 3:23–25; 5:9–10; D&C 76:40–42; John 3:15–17—Jesus Christ ransomed us through His Atonement.

John 5:22—Jesus Christ will be our judge.

Alma 7:11–12—Christ is the only one qualified to judge us justly because He has experienced all of our sins and trials.

Salvation through the Grace of Christ

Matthew 25:31–46—Eternal reward is determined by how we serve others (works).

Matthew 1:21—Christ saves us "from" our sins, not "in" our sins.

Matthew 10:22; D&C 14:7—Only those who keep the commandments and endure to the end will be saved.

Ephesians 2:8—We are saved by the grace of the atonement through faith.

Romans 8:24–25—We are also saved by hope.

Philippians 2:10–12; James 2:14–26—We must do our part by making and keeping our covenants if we expect to be saved from our sins.

Ephesians 2:8–10; Romans 3:19–31—Paul taught that we must rely on the Atonement and grace of Christ. Works in and of themselves avail us nothing without the saving grace offered by Christ through the Atonement.

2 Thessalonians 2:13—Exaltation can come only through our sanctification.

Hebrews 7:1–12; 8:6–13—It was through the Melchizedek Priesthood that Christ was able to do what He did. Perfection (sanctification) cannot come through the Levitical (lesser) Priesthood; we must obtain the ordinances of the higher priesthood.

John 17:6–11—Only those who become part of Christ's family have full access to the saving grace of the Atonement.

Judgment (Assignment to Degrees of Glory)

D&C 131:6—No person can be saved in ignorance.

John 5:28–29; Acts 24:14–15; Alma 11:40–45—The gift of the resurrection will come to everyone, regardless of their righteousness; it is a gift of grace.

Philippians 2:10–12; Romans 2:5–6; Matthew 16:25–27; 1 Corinthians 3:8—What we individually inherit is not freely given. We earn it through our obedience or lack thereof.

John 14:2–3; 2 Corinthians 12:2; 1 Corinthians 15:40–42—There are different degrees of glory in the resurrection.

D&C 76:50–113—Qualifications for each of the three kingdoms revealed.

D&C 76:30–49—The sons of perdition will not receive any glory.

D&C 88:96–99—Those who are worthy of either the terrestrial or celestial kingdoms will rise in the First Resurrection.

D&C 88:100–102—Those who are to inherit the telestial kingdom will not be resurrected until the end of the Millennium (the Second Resurrection).

D&C 19:1–20—Those who do not learn to obey the commandments while in immortality will remain in the grave during the Millennium. Meanwhile, their spirits will be sent to hell until they learn to be obedient to the laws of the kingdom that they will inherit. They must also suffer for their own sins because they refused to let the Savior's suffering cover them. When their suffering ends, they will be allowed to leave hell and will eventually inherit a degree of glory.

Election/Adoption

Genesis 12:3; Abraham 2:9–12—Abraham's family is set apart as God's family.

Isaiah 42:1—God upholds His elect.

Isaiah 45:4—Israel is God's elect family.

Isaiah 49:6—Salvation to come to the world through the house of Israel.

Isaiah 65:9, 22—God's elect will inherit eternal life.

Matthew 24:22; Mark 13:20—The Lord is mindful of His elect; they are chosen.

Matthew 24:31—God will gather His elect to inherit salvation.

John 15:16—God's elect are the chosen of the Lord and are called and ordained.

John 17:5–10—The fullness of the Atonement applies only to the covenant family.

Romans 8:17—God's elect are joint-heirs with Christ to the things of the Father.

Romans 9:11—The election is set forth before birth.

Romans 11:5—The elect are chosen and foreordained.

Colossians 3:12—God expects more from His elect.

1 Thessalonians 1:4—There is an election for eternal life made by God.

2 Thessalonians 2:13–14—People were elected before this earth life.

2 Timothy 1:8–9—A pre-earth election was held.

2 Timothy 2:10—Christ endured all things for the elect's sake.

Titus 1:1—God's elect have the hope of eternal life.

1 Peter 1:2—God foreknew His elect.

1 Peter 2:9—The elect are a called and chosen people.

2 Peter 1:10—We can become God's elect, even if we were not born as such.

2 John 1:1; D&C 25:1–3—Election is not gender specific.

Abraham 3:22–23—People were elected to different callings in the pre-earth life.

Revelation 7—Many will be elected to eternal life.

Book of Mormon

Mosiah 5:15—The elect are to abound in good works in order to obtain salvation.

Alma 13:3—The elect were called and foreordained.

Mormon 7:5–10—If people believe the Bible, then they should accept and believe the Book of Mormon, because it is part of the same story.

Doctrine & Covenants

29:7—The elect will hearken to the word when they hear it.

84:34, 99—We become the sons of God, His elect here in this life through the priesthood. The elect are to be redeemed through grace.

131:5—Our calling and elections can be made sure.

New Testament

Ephesians 1:4–5—We must be adopted into Christ's family, as His children.

Galatians 3:7, 29—Adoption into the Abrahamic covenant is necessary for salvation.

Romans 8:15, 23—If we are children of the adoption, we are heirs with Christ.

Romans 9:4–6—Paul explains the law of election.

Galatians 4:5—Saints become the children of God by adoption.

Eternal Life

Romans 6:8–10—Christ was resurrected; resurrection is eternal.

2 Corinthians 5:1–5—Mankind will be resurrected.

John 5:18–19—Christ is equal with the Father.

Philippians 2:5–6, 9—Christ being equal with God, is a God.

Acts 17:28–29—We are the literal offspring of God the Father.

Hebrews 12:9—God the Father literally begat our spirits.

Hebrews 1:1–4—Christ is God's heir of all things.

Romans 8:15–17—As God's children, we are joint-heirs with

Christ.

Philippians 3:13–15—Paul was seeking perfection and the high station of godhood; and he challenges us to do likewise.

John 10:34–36—The scriptures testify that we can become Gods.

2 Timothy 4:6–8; Psalm 82:1, 6—Many have attained godhood; as God's offspring each of us can become as He is.

1 Corinthians 8:4–7—God the Father is the head of the Gods.

Revelation 14:1—Many will attain the name of "God" upon their heads.

Revelation 7:2–10—There will be an innumerable concourse of Gods.

Hebrews 6:1–2—Perfection is attainable through the works of Christ.

Genesis 6:9—Noah attained perfection.

Genesis 17:1—God commands Abraham to be perfect.

Matthew 5:48; 3 Nephi 12:48; Deuteronomy 18:13—We are commanded to become as God is—perfect.

1 Corinthians 10:13—God does not allow us to be tempted beyond what we can withstand.

Revelation 3:4–5; 12:10–11—Through the blood of the Lamb we can overcome the world and become as He is.

Revelation 3:12—All who overcome the world will attain the name of God.

Revelation 2:7—We can attain eternal life with God and Christ.

Revelation 2:26–28—All that overcome will be given God's power to govern as He does.

Revelation 3:21–22—Those who overcome will sit on thrones as God and Christ do.

John 14:12—Those who are Christ's are given power to do all that he does.

John 17:14–26—Christ's adopted sons and daughters are one with Him in the same manner that He and His Father are one.

Hebrews 1:14—Angels will minister to those who become Gods.

John 12:26—God will honor all who choose to follow Christ.

Hebrews 3:14—We can be partakers of Christ.

Hebrews 9:15—All those who endure are given the promise of eternal life.

1 Peter 1:2–5—They who are sanctified through Christ's blood inherit salvation.

1 John 2:25—God promises eternal life.

1 Peter 3:18–20; 4:6; 1 Corinthians 15:29; Malachi 4:5–6—Those who died without hearing the gospel and receiving the saving ordinances will have the opportunity to accept them through the proxy work of the living.

Doctrine & Covenants

76:58–59—We can attain godhood.

93:6–28—Christ had to continue from grace to grace before attaining perfection.

132:18–20—We can qualify for godhood.

84:38—Through the Melchizedek Priesthood, we can inherit all God has.

88:107—Those who inherit eternal life will be crowned as Gods.

136:31—It is through overcoming our tests and trials that we can become as God and Christ are.

3 Nephi 28:10—Man can receive a fullness of joy equal with Christ and the Father.

Moroni 7:47–48—If we sanctify ourselves, when Christ appears we will be like Him, purified even as He is pure.

Covenants and Ordinances

Exodus 18:20; Leviticus 18:2–5; 2 Kings 17:37–38; Isaiah 24:5; Ezekiel 11:20; 43:11; Malachi 3:7; 1 Corinthians 11:2; Colossians 2:20; Hebrews 9:1, 10—God's people to live by His laws and ordinances.

John 3:3–5; 1 Corinthians 15:29—Baptism by the proper authority is required for salvation.

Book of Mormon

Mosiah 18:8–10

Alma 13:8; 30:3; 39; 50

4 Nephi 1:12

Doctrine & Covenants

1:15
88:139
107:20
121:19
124:33
128:8
136:4
138:58
131:1–4—Celestial marriage is required for exaltation.
132:15–20—Godhood is attainable through celestial marriage.

Perfection

Deuteronomy 18:13
1 Kings 8:61
2 Kings 20:3
1 Chronicles 28:9
2 Chronicles 15:17; 16:9; 19:9
Job 1:1; 8:20; 22:3
Psalm 37:37
Proverbs 2:21; 11:5
Isaiah 38:3
Matthew 5:48
Luke 6:40
John 17:23
1 Corinthians 2:6
2 Corinthians 13:11
Galatians 3:3
Philippians 3:12, 15
Colossians 1:28; 4:12
1 Thessalonians 3:10
2 Timothy 3:17
Hebrews 7:11–12; 10:1; 11:40; 12:23; 13:21
James 1:4; 2:21–22; 3:2
1 Peter 5:10

1 John 4:17–18
Revelation 3:2

Sources

Benson, Ezra Taft. *The Teachings of Ezra Taft Benson.* Salt Lake City: Bookcraft, 1988.

Doxey, Roy W. *Latter-day Prophets and the Doctrine and Covenants.* 4 vols. Salt Lake City: Deseret Book, 1978.

Encyclopedia of Mormonism. Edited by Daniel H. Ludlow, et al. New York: Macmillan, 1992.

Faust, James E. *Reach Up for the Light.* Salt Lake City: Deseret Book, 1990.

First Presidency Christmas Devotional. Salt Lake City, Utah, December 1986.

Hinckley, Gordon B. *Be Thou an Example.* Salt Lake City: Deseret Book, 1981.

———. *Stand a Little Taller.* Salt Lake City: Eagle Gate, 2001.

Hunter, Howard W. *The Teachings of Howard W. Hunter.* Edited by Clyde J. Williams. Salt Lake City: Bookcraft, 1997.

Hunter, Milton R. *The Gospel through the Ages.* Salt Lake City: Stevens & Wallis, 1945.

Journal of Discourses. London: Latter-day Saints' Book Depot, 1854–1886.

Kimball, Spencer W. *The Miracle of Forgiveness.* Salt Lake City: Bookcraft, 1969.

———. *The Teachings of Spencer W. Kimball.* Edited by Edward L. Kimball. Salt Lake City: Bookcraft, 1982.

Lee, Harold B. *Youth and the Church.* 3 vols. Revised. Salt Lake City: Deseret Book, 1970–73.

Maxwell, Neal A. *Wherefore Ye Must Press Forward.* Salt Lake City: Deseret Book, 1977.

McConkie, Bruce R. *Doctrinal New Testament Commentary.* 3 vols. Salt Lake City: Bookcraft, 1965–73.

———. *Mormon Doctrine.* 2d ed. Salt Lake City: Bookcraft, 1966.

———. *A New Witness for the Articles of Faith.* Salt Lake City: Deseret Book, 1985.

Millet, Robert L. *The Power of the Word: Saving Doctrines from the Book of Mormon.* Salt Lake City: Deseret Book, 1994.

Packer, Boyd K. *The Holy Temple.* Salt Lake City: Bookcraft, 1980.

Smith, Joseph F. *Gospel Doctrine: Selections from the Sermons and Writings of Joseph F. Smith.* Salt Lake City: Deseret Book, 1971.

Smith, Joseph Fielding. *Answers to Gospel Questions.* Salt Lake City: Deseret Book, 1957–66.

———. *Doctrines of Salvation.* Compiled by Bruce R. McConkie. 3 vols. Salt Lake City: Bookcraft, 1954–56.

———. *The Restoration of All Things.* Salt Lake City: Deseret News Press, 1945.

Taylor, John. *The Gospel Kingdom.* Deseret Book: Salt Lake City, 1943.

Wilcox, Amanda H. *Prophetic Sayings of Heber C. Kimball.* N.p., n.d.

Young, Brigham. *Discourses of Brigham Young.* Selected by John A. Widtsoe. Salt Lake City: Deseret Book, 1954.

About the Author

Douglas T. Bentley has taught seminary for twenty-four years in Utah, Arizona, and Idaho. A popular speaker at Especially for Youth programs, he has also taught missionary preparation classes at the St. George Institute of Religion.

After serving a full-time mission in the Washington Seattle Mission from 1976 to 1978, he earned an associate's degree from Dixie State College in 1979, a bachelor's degree in psychology from Southern Utah State College in 1981, and a master's degree in athletic administration from Idaho State University in 1987. He also received a Master of Scriptures certificate from the Church Educational System in 1998.

Brother Bentley, a licensed financial services agent, is the author of *Abraham's Seed and Covenant.* He and his wife, Deonn, live in St. George, Utah, and are the parents of four children.

9 26575 78375 2